I hope you enjoy
the book. Pete

# Almost Perfect

## How a Bunch of Regular Guys Built WordPerfect Corporation

W. E. Pete Peterson

**Prima Publishing**
P.O. Box 1260BK
Rocklin, CA 95677
(916) 786-0426

*To Marieta*

Production by Melanie Field, Bookman Productions
Copyediting by Jennifer Boynton
Typography by WESType Publishing Services, Inc.
Interior design by Bookman Productions
Jacket design by The Dunlavey Studio, Sacramento

**Library of Congress Cataloging-in-Publication Data**

Peterson, W. E. (Willard Eugene), 1949–
    Almost perfect : how a bunch of regular guys
built WordPerfect Corporation / W. E. Pete
Peterson.
        p.   cm.
    Includes index.
    ISBN 1-55958-477-7
    1. WordPerfect Corporation—History. 2. Word
processing equipment industry—Utah—History.
I. Title.
HD9801.U543U87   1993
338.7'61005'0979225—dc20                     92–34366
                                                                CIP

94 95 96 97 98 RRD 10 9 8 7 6 5 4 3 2

Printed in the United States of America

**How to Order:**

Single copies may be ordered from Prima Publishing, P.O. Box 1260BK, Rocklin, CA 95677; telephone (916) 786-0426. Quantity discounts are also available. On your letterhead, include information concerning the intended use of the books and the number of books you wish to purchase.

# CONTENTS

# ACKNOWLEDGMENTS

I would like to thank my first editor, Wendy, for reminding me that writing should be fun, and my subsequent editors Anne, Andi, Jennifer, Jennifer, and Melanie for not letting me look like I deserved all of those Bs and Cs in English. I also want to thank Will, Carol, André, Pam, Sam, Clive, Norm, Debbie, Devin, Julie, and Marieta for reading the unfinished manuscript and offering their suggestions. I am grateful to Bill for finding me a publisher, to Ben for taking a chance on the book, and to David Coursey for suggesting a great title. Finally, I want to thank my wife and children for putting up with me while I struggled to put the words down on paper.

# INTRODUCTION

On Monday, March 23, 1992 at 10:30 A.M. I walked into what I thought was a routine meeting of the Board of Directors of WordPerfect Corporation. Bruce Bastian, the chairman of the board, invited me to sit down in his office. Alan Ashton, the president of the company, entered the room and took a seat. The three of us had been the only members of the board of directors for the past ten years. We owned all the stock in the company.

Alan made it a point to tell me we were having a shareholders' meeting, not a board meeting. This seemingly small clarification was no minor detail. As with most companies, the shareholders of WordPerfect Corporation rarely met in an official capacity. When we did, it was usually to meet legal requirements rather than to address any serious business issues. The important decisions were made by the board of directors, even though it consisted of the same three individuals. A special meeting of the shareholders meant a change to the board.

Duff Thompson, our attorney, also joined the meeting. He repeated Alan's warning that we were having a shareholders' meeting, and gave us each a paper to sign to make sure the meeting was absolutely official. This did not look good to me.

Alan looked down at the conference table and recited from memory what sounded like a carefully worded speech. He and Bruce believed it was time for a change; they wanted to add three new members to the board of directors, so more people could have a voice in the important corporate decisions. Twice, I interrupted to try to clarify what was happening. After each interruption, Alan repeated his speech from the beginning, word for word.

Bruce then explained that some of my responsibilities had to go to other employees, so more people could make contributions. Specifically, my marketing and sales duties were to go to someone else. He made it clear I was still wanted on the board and in the company, but I would have to accept a different role. He said my influence was too great.

I felt numb.

When I started working with Alan and Bruce in 1980, their company had only six employees and sales of about $20,000 a month. By 1991, my last full year with them, we had more than four thousand employees and annual sales of more than half a billion dollars. More than ten million people worldwide used WordPerfect. The company had no debt, more than $150 million in the bank, more than $100 million in real estate, and millions of dollars worth of computers, cars, and furnishings. Our reputation was as impressive as our bank balance: Our customers loved our products; our employees never wanted to leave. We had built a business worth perhaps $2 billion, without the help of experienced business professionals, and without losing even a small part of the company to outside investors.

We discussed the proposed changes for almost three

hours, but the final vote was never in doubt. I owned 1 percent of the stock and Bruce and Alan each owned 49½ percent. Sales were down a little for the current quarter, and they had made up their minds. They no longer wanted me running their company.

I told them I did not want to stay if my marketing and sales duties were taken away: That would have taken all the fun out of my job. They argued that my other financial and management duties were important and that my contribution would still be significant. I would still be able to express my opinion and cast a vote on all important decisions.

Although I believed they were sincere in what they said, I could not stay. I did not believe a committee of six people could be effective, nor did I have enough energy left to try to make it work. If Bruce and Alan did not want me running their company, I was ready to leave. The past year had been a struggle, and twice I had written unsubmitted letters of resignation. They had paid me generously over the years, so I did not need the job for the money. I felt relieved. I was ready to let them find out what it was I did for them.

When they asked me to stay, I suggested a six-month trial separation, to give them time to determine whether or not they needed me. I insisted on a separation. They decided to sleep on it. (I naively expected them to ask me to come back within a few months.)

Two days later, Bruce and Alan accepted my offer to leave for six months. Although their decision hurt much more than I expected, I promised myself they would not see me cry. I hugged them both, wished them well, grabbed a few of my things and left.

When the six months were up, no one called to ask me back.

WordPerfect Corporation had been my life and my identity for twelve years. It was difficult to face that I was not a part of that company anymore. I could not wear my WordPerfect hat and my WordPerfect shirt on vacation and have people come up and tell me how much they liked our word processor. I was no longer an important executive who made difficult decisions that affected millions of people. I was no longer in a battle to the death with Bill Gates and Microsoft, spending almost every waking moment figuring out how to beat them.

I am proud of the small role I played during the early years of the personal computer industry. I was fortunate to have had the opportunity to be a part of WordPerfect Corporation's incredible success story, and except for the ending, my time there was perfect.

# 1

# INNOCENT AT BIRTH

___

While driving back to the drapery shop one afternoon in the summer of 1980, I had a strong feeling that one day I would be rich. I laughed to myself at this premonition. I did not care about being rich; I just wanted to pay the bills. My wife, Marieta, and I had four little children, a mortgage, an empty savings account, and a failing business. We were worried enough to wonder if it was time to disconnect the telephone and cancel the life insurance.

Our financial troubles resulted from the recession of 1980, when new home building in Utah County had stopped. I worked at Julie's Draperies, which I owned and ran with my brother, André, and my sister's husband, Lynn. During the week, I visited crazy housewives who called for appointments, giving them estimates for custom draperies and attempting to play the part of the talented interior designer. I called the housewives "crazy," because most of them went temporarily insane when they learned the cost of their window treatments. On Saturdays, I kept the books and wrote up the work orders from my sales. Sales for the year were only one-third, and my partners and I would go weeks without pay to keep the company afloat. Instead of five appointments per day, I now had only five or six per week.

With time on my hands and bills to pay, I took a job weekday mornings at a local supermarket, stocking the dairy case and bagging groceries. This kept me away from the drapery shop, where I often received sad and sympathetic looks from the women who sewed for us. The market paid four dollars an hour, which almost covered our house payment. I hated the job. I was supposed to stock the dairy case and bag groceries, but I mostly seemed to run back and forth between the two.

If I did not have a drapery appointment in the afternoon, I worked in our large garden with three of my children at my feet. Sam was almost five, Wendy was three, and Ellen was almost two. Joe was only a few months old; not quite old enough to know the fun he was missing. The garden was beautiful and weed-free and provided us with lots of food that summer.

Perhaps trying to get rid of all the dirt in our clothes was the reason our washing machine died. When it broke down and the repairman told us a new machine would be cheaper than fixing the dead one, my wife broke down too. Her father learned we did not have the money to buy a new machine and offered to pay for a new washer. We gratefully accepted his gift. Six months earlier we would have been too proud to take his help.

I spent a lot of my time that summer wondering what I would do if the drapery business failed. I had grown up expecting to earn a doctorate and do something important with my life, but after getting a B.S. in psychology at Brigham Young University (BYU) in 1972, I never made it back to school. After a year working as a bookkeeper for an employment agency back East, I returned to Utah and took a job in my mom's custom drapery business, thinking I would save a little money and then go back to school. When I met Marieta in 1974, getting married became more important to me than going to school. Once we started having children, I gave up some of my dreams and concentrated on making a living.

After my mom passed away in 1979, a lot of the fun went out of the business. She had had a talent for creating new designs and running the shop. In her will, she left one-third of the business to me, one-third to my brother, and one-third to my sister. I do not think any of us enjoyed owning or running a drapery business, but we were resigned to our fate. If not for the recession, we would probably all still be there, wishing we could find a way out.

As I considered my premonition on that afternoon in 1980, I tried to figure out how it might come true. It occurred to me that some of our relatives had money, and if they all died at once, we might inherit as much as $100,000. Considering our circumstances, that was an enormous amount of money, but my feeling did not seem to be about $100,000—the money involved would be more than I could count. Although I had no idea how such a thing could happen, I was impressed enough to tell my wife about the premonition later that evening.

I would not have imagined that one of our poorest relatives—my wife's brother, Bruce Bastian—would be the person to set the premonition in motion. I met Bruce in 1974, just a few weeks before I married his sister. He was then director of the BYU band, called the Incomparable Cougar Marching Band, and he was counting on his sister to perform with them. Once Marieta and I were engaged, she hung up her tambourine for good, so it took some time for Bruce and me to become friends.

Bruce earned his B.A. in music education from BYU and planned to spend his life directing a high school or college band. After graduation, he stayed at the university to work on an M.A. in music and to work part-time as a teaching assistant to the director of the band. When the director left, Bruce became acting director. The position was not permanent, and his pay remained at the level of a teaching assistant. He did not mind the low wages or lack of benefits, however—the band was his life.

Bruce cut an interesting figure at over six-feet-tall and 140 pounds, wearing his dark suit as he stood atop a ladder on the football field's fifty-yard line. Rarely one to smile, and with enough nervous energy to power the lights in the stadium, he was serious about his band and his music. He spent his summers writing the band's pregame and halftime shows, and he spent his spare time counseling band members when school was in session. He had a great band; they sounded more like a very large rock-and-roll group than a university marching band.

For his master's thesis, Bruce was writing a 3-D graphics computer program that displayed the band's step-by-step formations as they would be seen from anywhere in the stadium—from high up in the press box, from the end zones, even from underground. His thesis work was amazing for the time, especially since he needed to tie three computers together to get enough processing power to run his program. Given the demands of arranging the band's music, directing the band, and helping his students, his thesis progressed slowly.

At the end of the 1976–77 school year, the dean of the music department told Bruce that the school was hiring a new band leader, someone with a Ph.D. Bruce was extremely disappointed and was unimpressed by the dean's assurance that he was doing Bruce a favor. Fittingly, after Bruce left, the BYU band dropped the word *incomparable* from its name.

Bruce's thesis project, however, caught the attention of a BYU computer science professor, Alan Ashton. With Alan's help, Bruce got out of the music department and finished his M.S. in the computer science department.

He graduated in early 1978, and that spring, Bruce interviewed with many computer companies, including IBM, EDS (then owned by Ross Perot), and Hewlett-Packard. He leaned toward the job with HP until Alan talked to him about a new company he was forming to write word-processing software. Bruce liked the idea of working in a small company, so he took a chance, deciding to work for Alan.

Alan had begun work on a word processor in the summer of 1977. While he typically spent his summers consulting or teaching, for some reason nothing had turned up that year. Rather than do nothing, he spent his vacation designing a word processor, more as a mental exercise than as a conscious effort to start a software company. In the back of his mind, he hoped to one day find a way to bring his word processor to life and make, perhaps, an extra two or three hundred dollars per month from the effort.

At thirty-five, Alan looked the part of a college professor. His graying hair was usually a little too long, because he had trouble finding time to get a haircut. He and his wife, Karen, lived in a modest, three-bedroom house with their eight children. (They would eventually have twelve children, including a foster daughter.)

Alan's word-processing design drew on his earlier Ph.D. work at the University of Utah. The university's computer-science doctoral program was one of the first in the country and had attracted a number of now famous computer pioneers such as Bob Evans of Evans and Sutherland; Alan Kay, who would work at Xerox PARC and later become an Apple Fellow; and John Warnock, founder of Adobe. For his doctoral thesis, Alan used a computer to create music on a Hammond organ. Although this is taken for granted today, computers were not making a lot of music in the early 1970s. For music to sound like music, the notes have to be played at the right time, and computers back then were too slow to be very good at playing them promptly. As with music, word processing works best when things happen at the appropriate time. When you type a letter on the keyboard, you want to see it immediately; you do not want to wait around for the computer to fit your letter into a processing schedule. The techniques Alan used to make good music also helped him create a great word processor.

In 1977, word processing was still fairly new, so Alan didn't have to devote much time to research. After seeing a demonstration of a Wang word processor and reading an early word-processing study, he was ready to start. He already had some experience, because most of his consulting work and a lot of the research he did with his students concerned text processing. Text processing, or text editing, was a primitive form of word processing used mostly for writing computer programs.

Alan set out to design a product that was not the standard run-off word processor in which the text on the screen would not look like the printed text. (If you changed the margins, you would not see the margins change on the screen, but you would see the change when the document was printed.) Worse still, a run-off system used ugly codes like .LM12 or @HD@B in the middle of text to change how the document looked on the page. Alan wanted the screen to look like the printed page, with the correct line breaks and page breaks and without any ugly codes. This design would also eliminate the repagination step used by run-off systems. Because Alan's document was always formatted correctly on the screen, there was no need to reformat it for printing.

Alan's design included a number of innovative ideas. Instead of forcing users to look at only one document page at a time, Alan wanted them to be able to scroll through the document, as if there were rollers at the top and bottom of the screen. He used function keys for the different features, so he could keep menus from cluttering up the screen. He designed an automatic insert, so if the user typed text in the middle of a line, the new text would push the old text out of the way instead of erasing it, as was the standard for the time.

He also eliminated the different typing modes, a feature which plagued the early word processors. With other products, if you were typing new text at the end of a document, you had to be in a create mode. If you typed it in the middle, you had to be in an edit mode. In an edit mode, your typing would erase existing text, so to insert text, you had to change to an insert mode. Alan allowed the user to type anywhere in the document without a mode change.

By the end of the summer of 1977, Alan had a design specification of about fifty pages in length. His clean screen, automatic on-screen formatting, absence of modes, and auto-insert were great improvements over previous word processors. This design was, however, more a list of objectives than a comprehensive set of specifications. If he had been writing a symphony instead of a program, you would have said that he had a collection of melodies, short phrases, and ideas. Most of the work, including the arranging and orchestration, remained to be done. He gave his hoped-for product the unassuming name of WP and stored it away when school started in the fall.

The next spring, at the same time Bruce was about to graduate, Alan received a call from Don Owens. Don then worked for Itel, a leasing company in Northern California, and he had dreams of starting his own software company. His background was in marketing, and he was a typical entrepreneur, with lots of ideas and plans, but not a lot of money. Don had a forceful personality—the type of guy who would always have his sales quota booked well in advance of any deadline. He had heard of Alan because of some text-processing consulting work Alan had done for Hill Air Force Base. He asked Alan to write a word processor for Data General computers on behalf of a company to be founded, funded, and owned by himself and his friend Bob

Johnson. Alan was not sure of his position in the company, although he was under the impression he would own a part of it. In spite of the fuzzy ownership details, he was excited about the chance to bring his design to life.

Don named the new company Satellite Systems, Inc., because he liked the acronym SSI, which he had seen on the side of a railroad car. "Systems" was part of the name because he intended to sell computer systems as well as software. "Satellite" fit the acronym, but was a poor choice—not everyone could spell it, and it gave the impression the company sold television antennas.

Based on Don's promise to finance the business, Alan offered Bruce a job as a programmer. Together, they signed a lease for office space and ordered a computer. Bruce was married at the time, and his wife, Melanie, was expecting their second child. (Melanie worked for us part-time in the drapery business quilting bedspreads.) As soon as Bruce accepted the new job, they signed a mortgage on a home. The day after the mortgage papers were signed, Don broke the news that the project funding had fallen through. Don could come up with his share of the money, but his partner could not. Don felt sorry for Bruce and gave him a $100 bill to ease the pain.

Alan also felt bad, and he called some business acquaintances to help Bruce find work. He learned that Eyring Research of Provo, Utah, was looking for a programmer. He spoke with them, and they ended up offering Bruce a job. Once there, Bruce discovered that Eyring was under contract to provide a Data General computer to Orem, then a small city of about fifty-thousand people just north of Provo, where Bruce and Alan lived. Eyring had agreed to provide a word processor with the computer system.

Eyring's word-processing commitment described exactly the type of software Bruce and Alan had been planning to write for SSI. Knowing that Eyring would be hard pressed to provide a good word processor in time to fulfill its contract, Bruce and Alan went to Eyring with a proposal. If Eyring would be willing to pay Bruce's salary during the project, and if Alan and Bruce could retain ownership of the finished product, Alan would bring his design and his time to the project without charge. Eyring agreed to the arrangement, which gave it a much better chance of fulfilling the contract with Orem. Eyring retained rights to sell the word processor if it sold similar computer systems to other cities, but Bruce and Alan owned the resulting product outright.

Eyring's contribution amounted to only a few thousand dollars for Bruce's salary, but it was enough for Bruce and Alan to get started. Alan worked on the project practically every moment he was not teaching, including nights, holidays, and Saturdays. Bruce worked almost every hour he was awake, even though most of his friends and relatives told him he was crazy. Alan worked primarily on the part of the program which did the printing, and Bruce wrote the screen portion. Together, they improved and expanded Alan's original design. Bruce made many contributions not only to the code of the finished product, but also to much of its design.

By the spring of 1979, Eyring felt the program was ready to deliver to Orem, but Bruce and Alan let Orem know they intended to continue improving the program. Orem let them continue to use its computers without charge as long as they could upgrade to a new version without an additional fee. Bruce borrowed a little money from his father so he could continue full-time work on the project, and Alan continued to contribute his nights, holidays, and Saturdays without pay. They worked in the basement of the Orem offices for another year to make a version of WP they could sell commercially.

To raise enough money to keep Bruce's bill payments up-to-date, they decided to release a simplified version of WP. The abbreviated version, designed for program editing, was called P-Edit. Because neither had any experience selling software, they turned to Don Owens for help. They traveled to California to show

Don the product, and he quickly sold a few copies of P-Edit to his employer, Itel. Soon, the three agreed to start a business to sell P-Edit and WP, with each owning one-third of the new company.

Satellite Software International was incorporated in the state of Utah in September of 1979. The new name was very similar to the old one, since SSI was still their acronym of choice. (Back then, acronyms were even more popular in the computer industry than they are today. Some people thought it was more important to find a good acronym than a good name. Everyone wanted to be the next IBM, NCR, DEC, CDC, or HP.) "Software" replaced "systems," because the new company intended to concentrate on software instead of computer systems. "International" was added because it was impressive, and because the founders eventually hoped to sell software all over the world.

In March of 1980, the finished software, renamed SSI*WP, was offered for sale. Then, SSI*WP did not have nearly as many features as subsequent versions would, but the original product was very much like the DOS versions of WordPerfect. With a little thought and creativity, the user could make the features that were there do almost anything. The software came with a manual written by Alan and Bruce using their new word processor. The software's retail price was $5,500. The company's cost to manufacture a complete package, which included a computer tape, a manual, and a paper template, was about $25.

By today's standards, SSI's first word processor occupied a very small niche in the software market. The software worked only on Data General computers, only on DG's AOS operating system, and only with Data General terminals. To print a nice-looking document, the printer had to be a Diablo 1650 or work just like a Diablo 1650. While the niche was small, SSI had little competition and its product was very good. Bruce and Alan had paid close attention to the comments from secretaries and others who tested the product at Orem before it was released. SSI*WP was fast and easy to use.

By the summer of 1980, SSI was selling two or three copies of SSI*WP each month. Although the first sales were encouraging, Bruce was still not making much money. That summer, whenever he and his wife and children came over to our house for dinner, we would send them home with a huge garbage bag full of vegetables from our garden.

During those dinners, Bruce tried his best to explain to me what he was doing. My only experence with computers had come from a summer job in 1965, when computer time was very expensive and programs were written on punch cards. I had no idea how much computers had changed in fifteen years. His word-processing software seemed like a strange product to me.

Late in the summer, Bruce talked about the long hours he was working. During the day, he was answering phones, putting together information packets, and mailing them out; at night, he was writing software. I suggested he hire a part-time office manager to handle the phones and the mailings. He asked how much it would cost to hire someone, and I told him he could probably fill the position for about five dollars an hour.

Bruce called a couple of days later and asked me if I wanted to apply for the newly created job of office manager. Because the pay was five dollars an hour—a dollar more than I was earning at the supermarket—I quickly agreed to come to an interview, as long as he understood I could only work part-time. I still had hopes the economy would improve and the drapery business would recover.

I met Don Owens in early September, at my interview for the SSI office manager job. He spent more than an hour talking to me, showing me the help-wanted section in *ComputerWorld* and explaining the great opportunities available in the computer industry. He encouraged me to keep looking into computers even if I did not get a job at SSI. He sent me home with a few industry magazines and the promise that if I would read them, the stories would eventually start to make sense. About three weeks later, Don called, offering me the job. I agreed to start on October 1, on the condition I could quit as soon as the drapery business improved.

Although I did not know it at the time, that five-dollar-an-hour part-time job would turn into a great opportunity. Somehow, I had arrived at exactly the right place at exactly the right time. If Alan had found other work in the summer of 1977 or if Bruce had kept his job as band leader or if Don had decided not to start a business or if Orem had purchased an IBM computer instead of a Data General computer or if there had not been a recession in 1980, I would probably still be driving up and down State Street every weekday with drapery samples in my trunk. Like some rare astrological phenomenon when all the planets are perfectly aligned, all the necessary events came together at just the right time, and a new and soon-to-be successful company was born.

# 2

# THE BATTLE
# FOR CUSTODY

---

Starting a software company in the 1980s usually involved four rounds of financing. In round one, the founders used their own money—and money begged and borrowed from friends and relatives—to do market research and write a business plan. In round two, the business plan was shown to private investors to raise financing for product development. In round three, once a product was developed, the founders went back to their investors, and perhaps to a few new investors, for more money to pay for the product roll-out. (Roll-out is the process involved with introducing a new product—package and brochure design, advertising, press tours, sales strategy, etc.) If the roll-out was successful and customers actually bought the product, round four was the big payoff. The Initial Public Offering (IPO) was when everyone who contributed money in rounds one through three sold some of their stock to the public to make a bundle. By the end of the four rounds, the founders normally owned less than one-fourth of the company, but that was the price they paid for the chance to make a few million dollars right away.

SSI was not financed this way. Bruce and Alan skipped straight to round two—they went ahead with product development, despite having no idea of the size of their market or their chances for success. They financed the product development through their own work and with some help from Orem and Eyring Research. Don Owens was responsible for round three, product roll-out, and as with rounds one and two, it was done without asking investors for money.

Don Owens was a forceful salesman. He was about six-feet-one-inch-tall and had a large barrel-shaped chest. He did not give the impression of being overweight, but he looked like a guy who had played football in high school. He was gruff, stern, and not necessarily one to smile. Unlike Alan Ashton, who always flashed a big grin whenever you saw him, Don was all business. He dressed well, drove nice cars, and had a beautiful wife and two good-looking children. He looked the part of the shrewd and successful businessman. He loved to wheel and deal, and he knew how to close a sale.

Although $1,000 was carried on the books as the amount the owners originally contributed to start SSI, not one of them had actually invested any of his own money in the company. The thousand-dollar figure was pulled out of the air, because the real number was too hard to explain. As I understood it, the SSI bank account was opened with a $7,000 check made out to Don from Levi Strauss; it was his head-hunting fee for helping the jeans maker find a new employee. His $7,000 did not stay in the company for long, however. Within only a few weeks of the "loan," Don was selling enough software from his home in California to pay himself back.

Don's first customer was Itel, his employer. As mentioned previously, Itel was in the leasing business; one of the things they leased was Data General computers. They happened to use DG computers as well. In November of 1979, Don sold them a couple of copies of P-Edit, and in March of 1980, he sold them SSI*WP. One customer was all Don needed to get going. Using Itel as his reference account, he began talking to companies that used Data General computers, some of which were leasing clients of Itel. When one of them showed interest in the product, he would jump on a plane to go close the sale. Each time he made a sale, he asked for a letter of recommendation.

Once he had a few of these letters, Don used them repeatedly to promote SSI*WP. He sent them to computer trade publications along with his press releases. As the publications began mentioning the new product, he sent the letters and a one page brochure to companies responding to the news stories. If a company expressed more interest after reading the letters, he had Bruce send them a demonstration copy of the software.

Don always tried to sell the product for list price, but he was not afraid to make a deal if he had to. He was tenacious when it came to collecting the money, always extracting a promise of when the check would be mailed as soon as he made the sale. By June of 1980, Don had enough confidence in the new venture to quit his Itel job and move his family to Utah.

A few of the inquiries SSI received came from Data General's dealers. Data General sold some of its computers direct to customers and some through Original Equipment Manufacturers (OEM). This type of dealer purchased DG computers, added some software of its own, and then resold the computer/software system. The added software, or added value, theoretically made the DG computer into something new and original. At the time, DG did not want to sign resellers unless they added value to the DG product. I am not exactly sure why they formulated this policy, but back then the successful computer manufacturers were in control, and they tended to have a lot of dumb rules.

If a DG OEM showed interest in our products, Don asked them to pay full price for one copy and offered to sell them additional copies at a discount. The first copy had to be used in-house, meaning inside the company. The additional, discounted copies could be marked up and resold to the OEM's customers. The amount of the discount ranged from 10 to 80 percent, depending on how the negotiations went with each reseller. The discounted copies sold through resellers soon accounted for about half of SSI's sales.

Late in the summer of 1980, Don put together what was truly a big deal for SSI at the time. DCC, a communications company with offices in Memphis and London, was interested in writing its own word processor. DCC sold Data General computers, but instead of using DG's operating system, it used an operating system of its own creation. Although SSI*WP would not run "as is" on DCC's operating system, Don convinced the company to buy SSI's source code and use it as the basis for the word processor. His asking price was $100,000, and DCC agreed.

By the time I came in October, Don had enough reference letters and sales leads to insure a reliable cash flow. He had pulled off the impossible. Without raising any money and without spending a dime on advertising, he had successfully introduced SSI's products and established a reasonably good dealer network. The company was making enough money to pay decent salaries to its owners; to get them company cars; and to hire another programmer, a part-time bookkeeper, and a part-time office manager. (Alan chose a white Chevy truck with very few extras as his company car, which was very much in keeping with the twenty-nine-cent hot dogs he bought for lunch on his way from BYU to SSI most workdays.)

Bruce and Alan should have been elated with their success, but they were too tired to get excited. Bruce was still working fifteen-hour days, six days a week, and teaching one or two computer science classes at BYU. Alan now had enough money to fulfill his goal of finishing his basement, but he was teaching a full class load at BYU and spending at least forty hours a week programming for SSI. The new programmer, Dan Fritch, was hired not to lighten their load, but to write a new version of SSI*WP for another DG operating system called RDOS.

I was the sixth person to work at SSI, and the first person to quit. On my first day, the owners told me SSI did not withhold payroll taxes for any of its employees, and right then, I decided to return to the dairy case. My first rule of business was to have a healthy respect for the IRS.

Bruce, Alan, and Don asked me why I was quitting. I tried my best to explain the differences between an employee and a subcontractor, as well as the problems they faced by treating everyone as a subcontractor. They listened closely to my explanation and asked a few questions about basic bookkeeping and accounting. These questions turned into a job interview for the position of financial manager. Later that day, they offered me a full-time job for $24,000 a year starting November 1—with the promise that they would withhold taxes from my paycheck.

I immediately abandoned the drapery business. In theory, the drapery business paid each partner $1,500 per month, but that happened only when we could afford it. To keep the business going, we had to keep our expenses in line with sales. The only way we could do that was to pay ourselves only if we had the money. Some months we paid ourselves only half of the $1,500 to stay in the black, and one month that summer we received nothing at all. Two thousand dollars every month was more than enough incentive for me to move to SSI. My brother and brother-in-law tried to keep the drapery business going for another two years, but they could not make any money, even with one less paycheck to worry about.

Although my business knowledge was limited to what I had learned at my previous jobs, I was still an expert compared to the owners of SSI. The situation reminded me of a saying I had heard in South America while on a mission for the Mormon church; "In the land of the blind, the one-eyed man is king." Although the owners were very good at writing and selling software, none of them had had much experience running a business. They didn't withhold taxes; they hadn't held organizational meetings for incorporation; they had no corporate books. While they each claimed to own one-third of the company, they had nothing in writing and had not issued stock certificates. They had no business license (something Bruce discovered), and they had a bad habit of calling their expenses "miscellaneous," rather than keeping careful track of how the money was spent.

Before I joined the company, Bruce would spend twenty minutes or so every afternoon in line at the post office to mail the information packets. Too impatient to follow his example, I bought a little food scale and some postage stamps and, with a postal chart from the post office, set up my own little postal center in a closet at the office. This was a fairly remarkable thing in their eyes— to be able to mail small packages without standing in line.

Most of the things I did were very basic. I found an attorney to write the bylaws, as well as the minutes of the organizational meetings. I had stock certificates printed. I arranged for the owners to have wills written for themselves and their wives. I put together a monthly budget. I saw to it that a new phone system—with a real hold button—was installed.

It was not easy, however, to get the owners to withhold payroll taxes. Don had a friend who was an ex-IRS agent, and SSI paid him for tax advice. He disagreed with me about the owners needing to withhold taxes from their own pay, since Alan and Bruce were teaching at BYU and Don always seemed to have something else going. The ex-IRS agent changed his mind, however, just one week before the end of the year, when he heard a rumor that all subcontractors whose last name began with an *O* (like Don *O*wens) would be audited. We paid the FICA taxes in a lump sum at the close of the year, and luckily, the IRS levied no penalty.

My most enjoyable assignment during my early days at SSI was learning SSI*WP. Computers had changed a lot since I had last touched them. A few seconds at the keyboard was all it took to convince me that word processing was magical. Writing with a computer was at least ten times easier than writing with pen and paper. A year or so later, I would hear a Data General vice president say that a computer was at least as seductive as a beautiful woman, and I would understand what he meant. I was captivated.

The only hard part about learning SSI*WP was getting computer time. The company still used the Orem computer for most of its programming. We had only a small DG computer (small in power, but large in size) in the office, and Dan Fritch, the programmer for the RDOS project, needed it to do his work. Unlike AOS, which allowed many users to run many different programs at the same time, RDOS allowed you to do only two things at once. Since Dan liked having P-Edit and the assembler running at the same time, running SSI*WP was an inconvenience. It slowed him down, but for a couple of hours each day, he would use only P-Edit and let me use SSI*WP so I could get the letters and information packets out.

In January of 1981, I made what may have been my biggest contribution to the eventual success of WordPerfect Corporation. When the rough draft of the bylaws came back from the attorney, I noticed a three-fourths majority vote was required to elect or remove members of the board or officers in the corporation. Given the

distribution of the shares, this was the same as requiring
a unanimous vote to make any significant change in the
organization. On my own, I asked the attorney to change
the bylaws to require only a two-thirds majority, giving
any two of the shareholders the ability to control the
corporation. Don agreed to the bylaws without question.
He cared little for small details.

I suggested the change because the owners did not
seem very happy working together, and I was hoping to
give the company a chance to survive if the three ever
split. It was not in my mind to get rid of Don, but I
wanted Bruce and Alan to have some leverage if a battle
for control of the company were to take place.

The differences between the owners were substantial.
Bruce and Alan did not like Don's habit of calling himself CEO of SSI, since the three had agreed to run the
company as equals. They also did not like Don's ten-
dency to oversell the product. Once, a potential customer
called asking Don if we would support footnoting in the
near future. Don put down the phone (this was before we
had a hold button) and asked Alan when footnoting
would be ready. Alan said it would take six to nine
months. Don told the caller footnotes would be in the
product in three months. Alan heard the response and
was very angry—one of only three times I saw him angry
in twelve years. Don defended himself by saying he knew
the customer would like our product enough to wait
patiently for footnotes, an assumption which turned out
to be true.

Alan and Bruce were also a little discouraged by
Don's frequent habit of declaring bonuses for the
owners. There seemed to be a bonus for every occasion:
a Christmas bonus, a spring landscaping bonus, a back-
to-school clothes bonus. The most expensive bonuses
were given out when we got the first check from DCC for
$40,000. Don declared a $10,000 bonus for each owner
and a $6,000 bonus for Dan Fritch for helping with the
project. After the bonuses were approved, Don remem-

bered a $15,000 finder's fee owed to Verdugo Computers, one of our dealers, for introducing Don to DCC. Don went ahead with the entire amount of the bonuses, even though that left us $11,000 in the hole on the transaction. Bruce and Alan were happy to take their share, but they would have preferred to keep more of the money in the company.

The biggest disagreement between the three owners concerned financing. Don was impatient to get to round four and make a lot of money, but Bruce and Alan were not ready to sell stock to outsiders. Don seemed to be very discouraged to find himself stuck with partners who cared more about controlling their own company and products than they did about making money.

By the end of January, I had done everything I could think of to make us financially legal and proper, and I was running out of duties. Since I had time on my hands, Don made me a sales manager, even though I knew very little about selling software. I had never even heard of the word *schmooze*, a process very important to the job. You schmooze to make friends and build relationships, hoping to convince people to purchase your product or encourage others to purchase it.

I was beginning to feel comfortable around the computer after only four months on the job. Taking Don's suggestion, I was reading the trade publications for a few hours every night and acronyms like RDOS, AOS, VM/CMS, and MVS were starting to make sense. I was also learning how to mount tapes, initialize drives, and install software. The hardest part of becoming proficient with the computer was understanding all the new jargon. I would eventually see that most of the terms were descriptive and very unimaginative, but back then I was afraid of misunderstanding something. "Mount a tape" meant to stick a tape on the tape drive. "Initialize a drive" was a command to wake up a disk drive so it would be ready to do some work. What seems simple and straightforward now was very confusing at first.

I became a traveling salesman for SSI, despite my inexperience, because we had more companies interested in our product than we had people to travel. For my first trip, I was handed an airplane ticket and a reservation at the Hyatt Regency and was told to visit a law firm in Phoenix to answer a few questions and pick up a check. I made it to the law firm, answered the questions, and picked up the check without a hitch. When I later made it to the hotel, I was elated. I wasn't sure if I could figure out how to rent a car or check into a fine hotel, but I did both. I was awed by the sense of adventure and especially by the beauty of the Hyatt. I had a lot to learn.

Don asked me to go to Europe in February to train a new dealer in Holland and to meet with potential dealers in Switzerland. This was truly an adventure for me. In the seven years I had been married, I had spent only one night away from my family. Unfortunately, the trip was not all excitement and fun. I arrived in Europe in the middle of winter, and the dealer in Holland worked me sixteen hours a day. I did not see any sunshine for one whole week, because they picked me up at the hotel at 7:00 A.M., in the dark, and brought me back at 11:00 P.M. Staying in the hotel was lonely and boring. I lay awake for hours each night staring at the ceiling because the TV programs were all in Dutch, and I had not brought enough books to read.

The train trip through Germany to Switzerland was beautiful, however, and somehow I found my way to the right hotels and, eventually, to the DG office in Zurich. I would have felt good just getting to all the right places at all the right times, but luckily, I was also able to sign up a dealer from Bern and return home with a check in my pocket for $5,500. That was quite an accomplishment for someone who had never traveled abroad or read a train timetable before.

Although SSI*WP was available only in English at first, we had plans to create many international language versions. As we found dealers in various countries, we asked them to translate the program menus and help files into their native language so we could develop versions in those languages. We sold the translated programs with documentation in English, and in some cases we worked with our dealers to publish a translated manual. That DG customers had few word-processing choices made our job fairly easy in Europe.

We were rapidly becoming a big fish in the little DG pond. Businesses with DG computers could either purchase SSI*WP or they could purchase another computer. The other computers were called dedicated word processors, because they only did word processing. Since the cheapest dedicated word processor sold for about $15,000 per station, our software, which could be used by anyone on the DG computer, was a bargain at $5,500. Our problem was not price; our software was obviously much cheaper than the cost of another computer. Our problem was convincing customers that SSI*WP could fit on their DG computer without greatly affecting its performance. At the time, most of the computers used in business were purchased for accounting purposes, and the accounting departments were very reluctant to give others any time on them. If SSI*WP slowed a computer down or, worse, if it ever crashed a system, we lost a sale. Like guests, we were allowed to stay only as long as we were quiet and did not cause any trouble.

The profit margins in the software business were very different from those in the drapery business. The drapery business is very competitive, and we had to price our draperies within 20 percent of our cost to win half our bids. If even one customer did not pay us, we lost a lot of sleep. There was almost no competition in our small software niche, however, and we had no trouble charging thousands of dollars for a product whose materials cost little. Although there were costs for development, marketing, and overhead, we were still working on much better margins than most businesses, including many that are illegal.

As the year progressed, revenues grew and so did the number of SSI employees. Dan Lunt, who had done some contract programming for the company in 1980, came to work full-time at the start of the year. We had a receptionist and a part-time person who made tapes. We also started hiring a few BYU computer science students to work part-time. Our small offices behind the doughnut shop had filled up.

We were starting to get some competition by the summer of 1981. Our most aggressive competitor was a company in Northern California that sold a product called TIPS, an acronym for Text Information Processing System. By coincidence, the founder of the company was a classmate of Alan's from the University of Utah's Ph.D. program. Our other competitor was Data General, which was marketing a product called AZText. Although both were inferior, run-off products, we worried about TIPS because the company's salespeople seemed to stop at nothing to make a sale, and we worried about AZText because it had the support of Data General. Now that DG had a product of its own, we were considered a renegade and were no longer officially sanctioned.

As the summer wore on, Don did not come into the office more than a few days a month. He spent a lot of his time traveling, searching for investors, even though Bruce and Alan had told him repeatedly they did not want to sell additional shares. When he was in the office, he pushed hard for new features so we could stay ahead of the competition. He was also very negative about the future, and told me he thought we were headed for hard times because of our limited resources. More than once he talked of the need to raise money, hoping Bruce and Alan would change their minds. Don thought we might be able to sell part of the company for $3 million so each owner could walk away a millionaire. I wondered if he actually believed that our business would slow down, or if he was using that as an excuse to sell enough of the company's shares to outsiders so Bruce and Alan would end up owning less than half. I think Don expected any new investors to vote with him and let him control the company.

Don also started a new business with his wife and a friend from Washington, D.C., that sold terminals and printers to the federal government. When he was in the office, we began to wonder if he was selling software for us or selling terminals for himself, and when he traveled, we wondered if we were paying our expenses or his expenses.

The tension level increased as the months passed. Coming to work was a nightmare. Don would get upset if he wasn't involved in every sale, but it was difficult keeping him involved because he wasn't around very much. The contention made Bruce threaten to quit a number of times. Shouting matches were common.

Don asked me to move to Boston later in the year to become the East Coast sales manager. My primary duty was to build a closer relationship with DG, and I was to be paid a commission on all sales I made there. The job looked attractive because it got me away from all the stress. I was tired of being the person in the middle, trying to be loyal both to Don and to my brother-in-law.

My wife and I sold our home to Dan Fritch, and soon I was back in Boston looking for a house to rent or buy. I was there about four days when I started to have strong misgivings about the move. As I would drive around trying to find a good place to live, tears would stream down my face for no reason at all. I finally decided the move was a mistake, and I called the office to see whether I would still have a job in Utah if I returned. The extra money didn't matter. Boston was not the place for me and my family at that time. Dan did us a great favor by letting us out of our agreement to sell him our house.

Finally, Alan and Bruce decided it was time to ask Don to leave. They were tired of the fighting and felt they had plenty of excuses to end the relationship. They called our attorney for instructions. The attorney put together a script for a special meeting of the board, which was much like the meeting I would attend years later. I was at the meeting to take minutes, with instructions from Bruce to kick him in the leg if he lost his nerve. When confronted, Don was very repentant and said he would improve. Even though Alan and I kicked Bruce's shins repeatedly, he gave Don another chance.

Don promised to do a better job of working as a partner in a team, and I'm sure he meant it. It was difficult for him to change, however. Don was used to running things and he enjoyed being president and CEO of a successful software company. He was good at what he did and I believe he felt like he was being judged by the wrong standards, and that his results should have outweighed any shortcomings we perceived. I believe his personality was such that he could not work well with only one vote out of three, especially because it was Bruce and Alan who had the other two votes. To Don, they were programmers and intellectuals, not businessmen.

Despite Don's promise, conditions in the company didn't improve. Bruce and Alan called another meeting of the board at the end of the year to tell Don again that they did not want him to be one of the company's officers. They were willing to pay him as a consultant for one year if he would help with sales that were pending, but they did not want him coming into the office any longer. Surprisingly, Don agreed to their proposal, and the motion to remove him was passed unanimously. I think Don was convinced that they would regret their decision and ask him to come back in a few months, that he was in a "no lose" situation. The consulting contract paid him almost as much as his salary, and he still owned one-third of the company. If the company was successful, he would make money. If the company had trouble, he might have a chance to regain control of it.

We finished 1981 with sales totaling $850,000, more than double the $400,000 of the previous year. We had no idea how well we would do in 1982, but we were not too worried about the future. The struggle for custody was over; Alan and Bruce were in control of their company and their products once again.

In retrospect, Don's contribution to the company was worth all of the initial fighting. While I never understood why he was so eager to sell out, I did admire his ability to sell a product without spending a lot of money. I mentioned Don's departure to a customer later and tried to explain what had gone wrong. The client, who was a little older than me, would not let me say anything negative about Don. He said that some people are better at starting a business than they are at running a business, and that Don should be remembered for what he did, not for what we felt he should have done.

# 3

# CHILDREN MASQUERADING AS ADULTS

---

After Don left, we felt like little kids left on their own. We knew almost nothing about management or marketing, but we didn't care. We were free to do whatever we wanted to do, whenever we wanted to do it. The fighting was over, and as long as we didn't run out of money, we knew no one would bother us. We felt like we were playing "dress up," doing our best to look the part and imitating the way grown-ups played the business game.

If we had wanted to practice medicine, we would have needed a degree and some experience. If we had wanted to practice law, we would have had to pass the bar exam. Running a company, however, did not require proficiency tests, a college degree, or any relevant experience. While running a business *profitably* is arguably as difficult as any other profession, almost anyone is allowed to give it a try, whether they are qualified or not. It is like an inalienable right, available even to the foolish, the young, and the senile.

We never considered hiring professional managers to help us. In fact, professionals were the enemy. They represented "business as usual," which meant working for an overbearing boss, fighting political battles, and living with contention. A banker once suggested we look for someone with experience to run the company, so we found another banker. Having gained our freedom, we did not want to lose it. For my part, I enjoyed not having anyone look over my shoulder to make sure I wrote each letter correctly or said exactly the right thing to a customer.

Bruce and Alan asked me to take Don's place. Alan was to look after development, Bruce was to concentrate on our international business, and I was to do the sales and marketing for the United States and Canada, while keeping an eye on finances. None of us knew if I could handle it, so I started on a temporary basis, and if I felt comfortable, I could keep it. If I had trouble, I was supposed to help find someone who could do the job, and I would work under that person.

I asked company programmer Dan Lunt for his help because he had a technical background in computer science and engineering—something I lacked. I also thought that Dan's personality was better suited to marketing than to programming. He had trouble sitting in front of a computer eight hours a day. After a couple of hours of programming, he would wander around, interrupting someone or looking for something else to do. I was impressed with Dan's sales experience—he had sold real estate part-time for one year while he was in college. It was not until much later that I found out he had never even sold a house.

Dan and I didn't change much at first, except establishing a standard discount for all resellers. Running to the file cabinet to read a contract and find the right discount before quoting a price was not practical. As quickly as we could, we tried to give all our resellers a 40 percent discount, but it was not something we could do overnight. In some cases, it took us a few years to renegotiate the old contracts.

If we had had more experience, we probably could have found a lot of things that needed improvement, but we were doing well just learning what it was we were supposed to be doing. It took us a year to figure out how to run the business. Although our sales were not increasing significantly, our profits looked a lot better now that the large bonuses had stopped. We were never in any financial danger, with expenses averaging about $50,000 a month and sales averaging $65,000.

In spite of our flat sales, Bruce and Alan were not afraid to hire a few more programmers. Alan continued to teach at BYU, so he was in a perfect position to recruit its best computer science students. He was a tough grader, and anyone getting an "A" in one of his classes was a candidate for a job offer. When Alan found students with exceptional talent, he and Bruce would offer them part-time jobs and put them to work on one of the programming projects. By the time they graduated, their work had helped the company grow to the point where we could afford to offer them good salaries. We eventually used Alan's old grading records to search for good programmers who had already graduated.

Alan Brown was one of the BYU students we hired to work part-time. He was brilliant, especially at math, and he could do amazing things, like perform hexadecimal computations in his head. I think he had a photographic memory. He intended to go to the University of California at Berkeley after graduation to get an advanced degree and do research, but we hoped to be able to offer him enough money to change his mind.

His first "office" was the storage room, and he used a door stacked on some computer boxes for a desk. The boxes belonged to SSI's new IBM Personal Computer. The IBM PC had been announced late in 1981, and we bought one in February of 1982. Brown's first job was to see if it was possible to convert SSI*WP to run on the small IBM PC. Because there were no programming tools for him to work with at first, he did his initial programming in machine code. Programming in machine code is similar to eating rice with tweezers: both take a lot of time and patience. By March, however, Brown was convinced we could make SSI*WP work on the new computer, so we decided to go ahead with a PC project.

It was not a difficult decision. I remember when a few of us were eating lunch at the local Sizzler, an eavesdropper interrupted to say, "Are you guys writing a word processor for the PC? So are we." So was everyone else. At least two hundred companies would introduce a word processor for the IBM PC within the next two years. Most of these products never made money, because the market got very crowded very quickly, but our risk of failure was not as great as theirs. Many of our Data General customers were already planning to buy IBM PCs and hoping to use SSI*WP on them.

There were other small computers we could have supported first, like the Apple II or the Victor 9000, but the IBM PC seemed to have the greatest chance for success. IBM, especially in 1981, was well respected. They seemed big enough and powerful enough to do almost anything they wanted.

We would have liked to have had the first word processing product for the IBM PC—as someone said, "If you're going to march in a parade, you want to try to go in front of the horses."—but we had a number of hurdles to get over before we could put a lot of programmers on the project. Our first problem was whether to write the new version in assembly, which was the language used on the DG version, or in a high-level language like C, Pascal, or BASIC. Writing software in assembly language is somewhat analogous to baking from scratch rather than using a mix. The programmer has more control over the ingredients of his program if he uses assembly, but the programming requires more work and more lines of code than it would take with a higher level language. Most of the high-level languages were not well suited for writing a word processor, although we did consider using C. We had trouble, however, finding a reliable C compiler for the PC, and programming in a high-level language usually produced a bigger and slower program than assembly did. We decided to use assembly.

Once we made that decision, we were forced to wait until May for an assembler to come on the market. Once the assembler was available, we still needed a good program editor. EDLIN, the editor that came with DOS, was not worth using, so Brown began getting P-Edit ready to work on the PC.

In the meantime, the other programmers were keeping busy. They were improving the DG version, and by now we had released version 2.0 of SSI*WP. They added a lot of new features, including a spelling checker, footnotes, and some basic arithmetic that worked on columns and rows of numbers.

We had no systematic way of deciding what features went into a particular version of the product. Many of the improvements came from the suggestions of our customers, who were constantly calling with requests for more features. If something was easy to do and made sense, it usually made it into the next version. If it was very difficult or rarely requested, we would usually schedule the feature for a later release. Sometimes, if a customer absolutely had to have a feature right away, and if they were willing to pay a few thousand dollars to fund the work, we would take their money and move the feature to the top of the list.

While our software was getting better, our relationship with Don was getting worse. Even though we were paying him to be a consultant, we did not see him at all for the first few months of the year. After a vacation in Hawaii, he went to England as a consultant for his old employer, Itel. At Don's suggestion, Itel was starting a distribution company in Europe to sell software products for Data General computers. Don's plan to become a software distributor was ahead of its time. Eventually, software distributors would become the primary means of getting software out to dealers and customers, but to do it in Europe, in 1982, with software only for DG machines, gave Don little chance of success. There were not enough products or customers to support the venture.

Even though Don still owned one-third of SSI, he had his new company distribute our archenemy, TIPS, to its dealers and customers. As I remember it, he asked us for exclusive rights to sell SSI*WP in Europe, but when we dragged our feet, he decided to go with the other product. It was very strange to have a member of our board of directors promoting a competitor's word processor. We were not too happy to see press releases and TIPS sales literature containing Don's statements of endorsement for their product.

When Don came back to Utah for a short visit in April, we called a special meeting of the shareholders to remove him from the board of directors. Surprising us again, Don voted to remove himself from the board and nominated me to take his place. At the end of the meeting, he wished us well and encouraged us to make him rich. He told us some day we would pay him $250,000 for his stock. We offered him $30,000 on the spot, but he laughed. Don went back to England for a few more months, until his distribution venture was abandoned.

I liked my new role as a vice president and member of the board of directors of a young software company in a new industry. After years of wondering what I would do with my life, I had found my place. My job was so interesting and challenging that it consumed my every waking moment. I was past the point of being a workaholic. I would go to the office on Saturdays and stay much longer than was necessary. I would take piles of trade publications and literature home to read each night. I dreaded Sundays, three-day weekends, and vacations, since I could not go into the office. I was addicted to the software business and could not get enough.

In the spring, Dan and I decided it was time to advertise. We went to the local bookstore and bought a couple of books on advertising. After reading a bit, we wrote some copy and placed our first ad in a DG trade publication. When a few leads came back, we thought advertising was a snap. That was the first and last time we thought advertising was easy.

Our approach to advertising became our normal approach to doing all our business. Whenever we felt we needed to do something new, like pricing a product or working out a direct mail campaign (direct mail is the polite name for junk mail), we would buy a book, read a few chapters, and then do the best we could. We never thought to use an advertising agency, a public relations firm, or a consultant—Alan liked to repeat the joke that a consultant was a guy who borrowed your watch so you could pay him to tell you the time. Occasionally, we were willing to get help with legal and accounting matters, but never when it came to marketing, sales, or management.

If we had trouble finding a book on a subject, we tried our best to figure things out on our own. Figuring out how to sell our software so that we retained the legal rights to the product was one such problem. There were no easy answers and a lot of conflicting legal advice. Some lawyers suggested using trade secret law for protection; others thought copyright law applied; some suggested applying for patents. The situation reminded me of the times I was unprepared for an essay test in school. If I didn't know the answer, I would write anything and everything down in the hopes of getting at least part of the question right. Attorneys were doing the same thing. They didn't know the answer, so they suggested a little of everything.

In cases like these, where we couldn't figure out the

answers, we generally copied what IBM was doing. We would "license" our software, rather than "sell" it and try for copyright and trade secret protection. We granted the customer limited rights to use the software, but not to own it. No one knew if this arrangement would stand up in court, but it was the best decision we could make at the time.

We finally moved from our cramped space behind the doughnut shop into what—for us—were some very impressive offices. Novell, which started out in Orem as a computer manufacturer, was losing money and had decided to move to a less expensive location. We moved into Novell's vacated offices, enjoying their new wall-paper and carpet.

I went to my first DG reseller conference at about the same time. (This was also my first stay at a resort hotel—the Camelback Inn in Phoenix.) I enjoyed the speakers and the beautiful surroundings. There was so much interest in SSI*WP that people followed me everywhere—even to the men's room—to ask about it. We were having no trouble winning sales away from TIPS and AZText.

However, while our customers and dealers seemed to love our product, we did not get a lot of respect from the experts. Occasionally, a consultant would stop by the offices to take a look at the product, usually because a hardware manufacturer was looking for a word processor to purchase and call its own. Very few of these consultants liked SSI*WP. They would ask stupid questions like, "It doesn't look anything like Wang's, so how do you expect to sell it?" It drove me crazy that they rarely knew how to type and never took the time to learn how to use our product—after a quick look, they filed us away in their "losers" folder. Their lack of respect gave us motivation to work harder and prove them wrong.

Although we didn't understand it at the time, we were one of many small companies disrupting the established practices of the computer industry. As one consultant put it, we were a renegade company. Our product was strong enough that some DG resellers (not DG itself) were going after word-processing bids with Data General machines and SSI*WP. On a very small scale, we were starting to take business away from established word-processing vendors like Wang, NBI, and IBM.

The profitable, well-established computer manufacturers like IBM, Digital Equipment Corporation (DEC), Wang, Hewlett-Packard, and Data General were not accustomed to having outsiders come in and talk to their customers. In fact, the standard purchasing process followed by customers and vendors made it almost impossible for new or small vendors to sell their products. Customers did not decide to buy a computer system one day and simply pick it up the next. First they sent out an RFP (request for proposal) or an RFQ (request for quotation) inviting interested vendors to submit bids. The request contained a list of requirements for the system. The manufacturers would read the requirements carefully, and if they thought their system qualified, they would submit proposals and price quotations. Usually, one of the manufacturers was a "favorite" going into the bidding process, and it would try its best to get the customer to specify requirements most favorable to its system. This was one of the reasons IBM salespeople spent so much time getting to know their customers. The vendor that helped write the RFP could usually tip the odds of winning the bid in its own favor.

The proposals that the customer received rarely contained a mixture of products from more than one vendor: IBM sold only IBM products, DEC sold only DEC products, etc. Since the customer expected the system to work, vendors did not want the bother of mixing and matching a group of incompatible products. The proposals included hardware, software, systems engineering (any special programming services), training (teaching the customer's employees to use the system), support (answering questions from the customer's employees), and maintenance (regular servicing to keep it running smoothly and repairs when the system stopped running). This was one-stop shopping.

Once the proposals were in, the customer and the interested vendors went through something like a mating ritual, filled with meetings, presentations, demonstrations, promises, and a few rounds of golf, until finally one vendor was awarded the bid. Price was generally not the primary consideration. Though an IBM computer could be as much as twice the price of a comparable DEC computer, and a DEC computer could easily be twice the price of a comparable DG computer, IBM outsold DEC, and DEC outsold DG. Reliability was more important than price, and the winning vendor, of all those that filled the requirements, was usually the one with the best reputation.

Once the bid was awarded, the customer and the computer vendor were bound to each other forever, or at least until the next RFP cycle. A detailed contract governed every facet of their relationship. If the customer thought it might want to add something new to the system in the future, the contract required the customer to get permission from the vendor. Typically, any warranty or representation of reliability was voided with any unauthorized addition. And even if the vendor gave its permission for something new from a third party, such as SSI*WP, the vendor usually blamed any subsequent problems in the system on the added software or hardware. This is one reason we had to be so committed to customer support from the beginning—we always had to prove we were not the culprit if a problem developed.

The customer paid a high price for the reliability and convenience of one-stop shopping. In general, a vendor wouldn't make all the system's components: It would take other companies' products and private-label them. (In private-labeling, a vendor would put its own label on the outside of another manufacturer's product and sell it as its own.) To buy a NEC printer from NEC might cost

$2,500, but to buy the identical printer from Data General with a DG nameplate might cost $5,000.

Our existence and success were a threat to these cozy relationships and high prices. Instead of pushing customers to buy a new computer, we tried to convince them to add our software to their old one. Luckily, Bruce and Alan had chosen to create SSI*WP on a Data General machine. DG struggled against DEC and IBM to win bids, so they were more willing to allow a third party to get involved. So we were both ally to and enemy of DG, which accounted for the love/hate relationship we had with them through the years. We had to tread very lightly, being very careful about what we did and said around their customers to receive their cooperation.

As the largest and richest company, IBM benefited the most from the old way of doing business. Ironically, IBM was probably the most responsible for bringing down the old establishment. By going outside IBM for the operating system for their new PC, they opened the door for other vendors to sell to their customers.

The operating system (OS) is the first piece of software that runs on a computer. This software does just what its name describes—it operates the system. The OS software controls all the pieces of the computer—the processor, the screen, the keyboard, the disk drives, etc. If you turned on a computer that didn't have an operating system, nothing would happen; with an operating system, the computer comes to life and is ready to run other software. Other software products, which ran "on top of" the operating system, were usually called applications.

In the single-source, one-stop shopping old guard, almost every computer manufacturer wrote its own operating system, essentially guaranteeing that a computer from one manufacturer would never be compatible with one from another manufacturer. It was these incompatibilities that helped perpetuate the single-vendor solution.

Possibly because they were in a hurry to get their PC out the door, IBM decided to look outside for the PC OS. CP/M from Digital Research, the most popular OS for small computers, was the logical choice, but Digital Research somehow dropped the ball when IBM came calling. Bill Gates and Microsoft picked up the ball, buying rights to an OS very similar to CP/M and then adapting it for the IBM PC. IBM bought the PC operating system from Microsoft, but still allowed Microsoft to sell the same operating system to other companies, opening the door for other companies to copy their machines. Eventually, the same computer would be available from a number of vendors, giving customers the chance to shop around and get more competitive bids. The IBM PC turned the computer establishment upside-down. Microsoft, then a little software company near the bottom, would one day end up on top.

By August of 1982, Alan Brown had P-Edit working, and all of our programmers, including Bruce and Alan, started on the PC version. They targeted November 15 as the earliest possible release date and worked almost around the clock to finish the program quickly. The PC version was almost identical to the DG version, except that it didn't need the code to handle multiple users. We also changed some of the DG version's more violent terms—such as *abort* and *kill*—to less violent words such as *stop* and *cancel*.

We were in a hurry to get the program ready. Throughout the summer, we watched as product after product was introduced. EasyWriter, from Sorcim (their name came from the word *micros* spelled backward), beat us to market with IBM's help and blessing. IBM worked with Sorcim to get Easywriter ready early, and the company sold the product under its own name. In this case, the timing advantage didn't matter, because both versions were bad and bombed immediately. Volkswriter, a low-priced word processor, captured the low end of the market. Because the program had a very limited number of features, its programmer had used Pascal, which was available before the assembler, without worrying about the program's size.

Micropro's WordStar came out around the middle of the year and immediately captured a large share of the market. It had been the most popular product for CP/M machines, and now became the most popular product for the PC. WordStar was released early, mostly through luck. The programmer who had written it for CP/M had already left Micropro by the time the PC came along. Rumor had it that the Micropro programmers assigned to translate WordStar had a difficult time understanding the CP/M assembly code, so they did a quick and very literal translation to PC assembly. It was similar to translating a book word for word from one language into another, without trying to understand the meanings of the sentences. It was hard to believe, but the translated program worked, although it had a few bugs. By the time we came out with our PC product, WordStar owned at least 75 percent of the market; the twenty or so other word processors already on the market shared the rest.

One big problem we had getting ready for the PC release was finding a new product name: SSI*WP wasn't very catchy. I liked the name WordPerfect, but I couldn't get anyone to support me. I had thought of the name while pulling into a parking space in front of our offices, in one of those "Ah hah!" types of experiences. I liked the name because it reminded me of the phrase "letter perfect," used to describe something which was word-for-word correct. I rushed into the office, sure that everyone would go crazy and love the name, but no one did.

Months passed. We still could not agree on a name, so we held a contest among the employees. Whoever came up with the winning name would win $100. From a long list of nominations, we all voted for our favorite. Word Plus and ProWrite received the most votes, and WordPerfect came in somewhere near the bottom. In spite of a very poor showing, I put WordPerfect on the list of names we gave to the attorney for a trademark search, just in case we could not use one of the winning names. It turned out there was already a word processor with the name Word Plus, and there was a printer with the name Prowriter. Because we had taken so long to decide on a name, we had too little time to start over. Under these circumstances, WordPerfect became the unpopular winner. The name was so unpopular, in fact, that no one even paid me the $100 prize money.

Despite its initial unpopularity, the name proved to be a good one. It was so positive sounding that it made any criticism sound untrue. It was like naming a soap Makes You Look Younger, so the competition would have to say something like "Use our soap instead of the Makes You Look Younger soap." "WordPerfect" also sounded like a very good product.

That fall, I called on ComputerLand's headquarters to see if they were interested in carrying our product. Their chain of franchised stores was the largest and most important part of IBM's distribution channel at the time. We were willing to offer ComputerLand an exclusive right to sell the PC product if they would promise to pick us up, but, luckily, the buyer I talked with was not interested in the offer. I did ask him, however, how many copies a moderately successful product might sell in their stores. The buyer said they had very few moderately successful products. They generally had only hits and misses. A miss sold almost no copies, but a hit could sell two to three thousand copies a month. As he spoke, I quickly did the math in my head. Three-thousand copies was about $500,000 a month. I could not imagine getting that much money from just one customer.

Dan took charge of advertising and planned to have advertisements in the PC magazines on October 15. This was a little early, but back then it was a common practice to advertise a product before it was ready to release. Some companies went so far as to advertise software even before they started the programming work, making sure they had orders before they made their development investment. At least our software was close to completion when we ran the advertisements.

At Bruce's insistence, we committed all our savings to the ad campaign announcing WordPerfect 2.20. I remember how dramatic and daring it seemed when he said, "We'll spend $100,000 on the roll-out if we have to." The ad we came up with looked like the cover of a science fiction magazine. It had a lightning bolt coming out of a man's head, going through his hands, continuing through a computer keyboard, and writing words on a piece of paper. The ad was beautiful, but it could have used some professional help. We were amateurs, and it showed.

We officially announced the product with a mailing to dealers and the press on October 15. Terry Brown, an old friend who was hired in 1981 to help with documentation, prepared the mailing. He also tried to get the manual ready to go to press on November 1.

When WordPerfect actually started working on November 18, there was little time to celebrate. There were a lot of bugs to get out, and the speller and "sort" features were still not finished. At the last minute, Dan decided we had to have an Epson printer driver (the Epson printer was one IBM sold for the PC, with its own label), so he went back to programming for a few days to write the driver.

WordPerfect 2.20 for the IBM PC shipped the day after Thanksgiving. It was a good thing WordStar was number one, because we could not have handled a large sales volume. We did not know how to assemble packages or how best to ship them. We did not take the time or spend the money to have a typeset manual or plastic keyboard template made. There were many things we had to learn before we would be ready to take over the market.

If somebody wonders whether they have a first edition copy of WordPerfect for the PC, they can know for sure because the first five or six pages look like bad photocopies. Just moments before WordPerfect was supposed to ship, we found some problems with the installation instructions. At the last minute, we typed up new pages with the word processor and then photocopied, cut, punched, and put them in the binders.

Our entire manufacturing facility fit in a room about twenty-five-feet square, and we were still a small company with only eighteen employees. We purchased a couple of disk duplicators, but the machines couldn't keep up with our orders. For the first few weeks we caught up by paying our older kids a dime a disk to duplicate the disks at home. We also hired Alan's daughters to put the replacement pages in the binders until the new manuals were ready. Alan was still coming in after hours with his older kids to clean the offices for extra money.

Our orders department consisted of two people taking orders at desks in the hallway at the center of our building. We put some shelving up on the wall across from where they sat to hold the ready-to-ship packages. With the order desk in the middle of everything, we all knew what was happening. We all liked to watch as the manufacturing people, led by Dan Lunt's brother Ron, assembled the packages and placed them on the shelves. We knew how well sales were going by the height of the stack of invoices on the order desks and the number of boxes waiting to be picked up. If manufacturing fell behind, we all pitched in to help them catch up. It was an exciting time.

I remember the first WordPerfect sale. I had come into the office for just a few minutes on the day after Thanksgiving, and as I was walking out the door, the phone rang. I picked it up on impulse. A man at the other end of the line said he had seen our ad and asked to buy a copy of the program. As I wrote down his credit card number and his address, I was thinking how much easier it was to sell PC software than DG software. The experience was almost intoxicating.

Despite the crowded word-processing market, our weird ad, and our cheap-looking manual, our phone seemed to ring off the hook. Sales for the last quarter of 1982 jumped from a quarterly average of $200,000 to $450,000. We finished the year with sales of a little over $1,000,000. That was not much more than the $800,000 we had made the year before, but we had done it on our own, without Don's help. By trial and error, we had learned how to sell our DG products and how to introduce a PC product. We were only a small group of friends, relatives, and neighbors with little experience, but we were profitably running a million-dollar business and having a good time.

Our peaceful existence as unsupervised kids was about to come to an end, however. The stable, slow-growing DG business was about to be overrun by a very unstable and rapidly growing personal computer business. Soon, we would not have the luxury of solving problems and making decisions at a leisurely pace in an isolated environment high in the mountains. We would have to grow up quickly to keep up.

# 4

# STARTING SCHOOL

---

Back in my drapery days, I used to lose a lot of sleep thinking about all the deadbeats who owed us money. One guy in particular made me very angry. He ordered and received a houseful of drapes and then refused to pay, claiming I had promised him the drapes as a favor. We tried to get help from our collection agency, but discovered that he was a disabled veteran; his pension from the military, which was his only source of income, by law could not be garnisheed. Occasionally, I would see the man in the grocery store, and each time my frustration would return and I would lose a few more hours of sleep.

It took me seven or eight years to realize that my anger was not helping the situation. I needed to grow up and accept that a small percentage of customers were going to try to find a way to avoid paying for their drapes. Losing a little money to deadbeats was just one of the costs of doing business. I learned to hand the deadbeats over to the collection agency and then forget about them.

When Don Owens started selling TIPS in Europe, we were similarly angry. How could we let a major shareholder—who knew our business inside and out—work for the competition? We wanted him out of the company immediately, but his asking price of $250,000 was more than we could pay.

We were young in terms of business experience, but we were smart enough to go to a good law firm for advice. Our attorneys suggested we dilute Don's holdings as a way of urging him to settle for a smaller amount. Key to a legal dilution was the old agreement Bruce and Alan had with Eyring Research—the agreement which clearly showed that Bruce and Alan were the owners of the word-processing software. Although Don may have felt otherwise, Bruce and Alan had proof that they had never given ownership of their software to SSI. This claim put SSI in a very difficult position. If SSI only owned the right to sell and enhance the software, then Bruce and Alan were in a position to revoke this right. Luckily for SSI, Bruce and Alan were willing to sell their ownership rights to SSI in return for a big chunk of stock. Unfortunately for Don, the effect of the sale would be to decrease his percentage of ownership in the company.

Our attorneys expected Don to be very unhappy with the transaction, but they also expected him to realize eventually that he could not legally stop or reverse it. The attorneys hoped that once Don owned a significantly smaller share of the company he would sell out for a smaller amount. The possibility existed, however, that Don would bring a lawsuit against us all. The thought of being sued was a little frightening to me, because I did not yet realize that lawsuits, like deadbeats, were a normal part of doing business. I did not understand that a successful company was always bound to have at least one or two lawsuits against it.

Our attorneys did their best to educate me in the ways of the real world. They explained that running a company was a lot like running a ranch in the Old West. Back then, a rancher could not count on the judicial system to protect his interests, so he had to enlist his own hired guns to protect his property. If a rancher was weak or had no stomach for a fight, rustlers would steal his cattle and tougher ranchers would take his range. Likewise, if we had no stomach for a fight, our software would be stolen, our trademarks infringed, and our savings taken by customers claiming harm from our products. If we did not use our hired guns (our attorneys), our judicial system would not protect our interests. We were fast becoming a company with deep pockets, and we had to be willing to fight to prevent people from emptying them.

I was not ready to believe the attorneys at the time: I was still too young and too idealistic. Unfortunately, what they were telling me was true. Even if a successful company is fair and honest in every one of its business dealings, there will be a few lawsuits. The only way to avoid them is to stay unsuccessful and keep your pockets empty. As soon as you have something worth having, there will be someone else who will try to take it.

It was a hard decision to risk the lawsuit with Don, but Bruce and Alan were upset about his helping the competition. Once we went ahead, the first step was to have an independent party appraise the value of the software as well as the value of SSI. Next, Bruce and Alan made a formal offer to sell their software, which was appraised at about $500,000, to SSI in return for more stock. A special meeting of the board of directors was called in the summer of 1982 to consider the offer. Although Don was no longer on the board, he was invited to the meeting so he would know exactly what was happening. Naturally, he objected to the purchase, but the board voted to proceed. Don had walked into the meeting owning one-third of the company, and had walked out of it owning only 5 percent.

Don sued SSI and those of us on the board as a result of the sale. Throughout the fall and winter, depositions were taken and settlement offers and counteroffers went back and forth. I came to view my first deposition as a rite of passage. It was time to start growing up a little.

By January, we were very anxious to settle the lawsuit. I asked the attorneys to do whatever they could to negotiate a settlement right away, before we were required to announce our software sales. We were now offering Don $100,000, and he was asking for $150,000. We increased our offer to $139,000, and Don accepted, agreeing to sell his stock back to SSI and drop his lawsuit. We only had $139,000 in the bank, but it was certainly a bargain considering what WordPerfect Corporation would be worth in a few years.

After the settlement, Bruce and Alan each owned 50 percent of the SSI stock. Not too much later, they let me buy 0.2 percent of the company. They talked about offering me more stock, perhaps as much as 10 or 20 percent, but I wasn't interested. I was worried that one of my in-laws might someday claim that I had taken advantage of Bruce. I wanted only enough stock to be a tie breaker, in case Alan and Bruce were to disagree or one of them were to die. SSI loaned me the money to buy my 0.2 percent of the shares, and I wrote and signed a buy-sell agreement that gave the company the right to buy back my shares at the price I had purchased them. I did this because I did not want anyone to question my motives. Actually, I never even used my vote to break a tie. In the years we were on the board together, I cannot remember an occasion when Bruce and Alan disagreed. Decisions were always passed by a unanimous vote.

Sales for the first quarter of 1983 were slightly higher than the previous quarter, proving that our record fourth quarter of 1982 was not a fluke. Almost overnight, our PC product had doubled the size of our business.

While we did not have a large share of the PC word-processing market, our expectations were so low that we thought we were wildly successful. Success is, after all, measured by expectations. Had we known more about playing the software game, we could have done far better that year.

We learned a lot from watching Lotus do it the right way. They spent about $500,000 developing 1-2-3, which was approximately the same amount of money we spent to develop the DG and PC versions of WordPerfect. They spent about $2 million on their 1-2-3 roll-out; their ads, brochures, packaging, distribution, and public relations were all very professionally done. We had spent only $100,000 on our roll-out, however, and generally looked like amateurs at everything we did. 1-2-3 became the most popular spreadsheet as soon as it was released. We would need five years to become the most popular word processor.

Watching another company, Softword Systems, Inc. (another SSI), also taught us some valuable lessons. They developed a PC word processor for an insurance company back East and then released this product to the public early in 1983. Their word processor, first called WordMate and later MultiMate, was designed like a Wang word processor. Wang apparently did not object to the copycat product, perhaps because it had a multibillion-dollar hardware business and was not interested in bothering with a multimillion-dollar software business. This other SSI would do $10 million in sales in 1983, outselling us almost three to one with what I thought was an inferior and outdated product.

My marketing department was mostly to blame for our comparatively slow start, but part of the problem was our software. Our biggest software shortcoming was its lack of printer support. While our Diablo support was very good, our Epson driver was a "kludge" (a kludge is a makeshift solution that is usually poorly designed and unreliable), and our support for all other printers was minimal. Early reviewers also complained about our paper keyboard template and unprofessional-looking manual. We were able to correct the problems with the template and the manual early in the year, but the printer support would not be fixed until the release of version 3.0 the following year.

Another serious problem was our growing reputation for buggy software. Any complex software program has a number of bugs that evade the testing process. We had ours, and as quickly as we found them, we fixed them. Every couple of months we issued improved software with new release numbers. By the spring of 1983, we had already sent out versions 2.20, 2.21, and 2.23 (2.22 wasn't good enough to make it out the door). Unfortunately, shipping these new versions with new numbers was taken as evidence by the press and by our dealers that we were shipping bad software. Ironically, our reputation was being destroyed because we were efficient at fixing our bugs.

Our profits were penalized as well. Every time we changed a version number on the outside of the box, dealers wanted to exchange their old software for new. We didn't like exchanging their stock, because the costs of remanufacturing the software and shipping it back and forth were steep. This seemed like a waste of money, because the bugs fixed were minor and did not affect most users.

Our solution was not to stop releasing the fixes, but to stop changing the version numbers. We changed the date of the software on the boxed diskettes, but we left the number on the outside of the box the same, an industry practice known as "slipstreaming." This was a controversial solution, but our bad reputation disappeared. We learned that perception was more important than reality. Our software was no better or worse than it had been before, but in the absence of the new version numbers, it was perceived as being much better.

Because we had such a small market share, we missed

out on the biggest opportunity of 1983, the panic-buying by hardware companies. IBM's personal-computer success led to reckless efforts by other hardware companies—DEC, Hewlett-Packard, Tandy, Data General, and others—to come out with their own PCs. Since these companies were afraid of copying IBM's PC exactly, and perhaps because they felt they could make better PCs, their new computers were not completely compatible with IBM's. The incompatibilities meant that IBM PC software applications would not run on the non-IBM machines. Because software is essential for a computer to be successful, the hardware companies were eager, if not desperate, to pay the most popular software companies to translate or "port" their programs' code to the new machines' operating systems.

Hardware company representatives hurried from one successful software company to another, handing them their money. The waiting rooms of the software companies were like crowded butcher shops; customers had to take a number and wait their turn. VisiCorp, the publisher of VisiCalc, was either so busy or so arrogant that it forced the hardware representatives to wait weeks for appointments. When Lotus announced it did not intend to port 1-2-3 to other machines, but instead would introduce and port a new product (called Symphony), rumor had it that the hardware companies were paying a combined up-front fee of $32 million for rights to sell the unfinished and unproven product.

No one waited in our lobby, however. Data General came by to purchase a few copies of our IBM PC software for its machine, but it was the only hardware company to do so. We were, at best, a second-tier company with unknown products. There was some money available to second-tier companies from a number of the lesser-known hardware companies, but many wanted to include software with the purchase of their computers, but the going rate for this bundled software was at most 5 percent of the retail price for a complete package. A twenty-five-dollar price seemed like an insult, and we were neither hungry enough nor desperate enough to give our product away.

Although we didn't receive a windfall from all the crazy porting and bundling activities of 1983, we were porting our software to many of the non-IBM MS/DOS machines anyway. We made versions for the Victor 9000, the DEC Rainbow, the Tandy 2000, the TI Professional, and a few others, while other companies were demanding large fees or declining to port their products to these machines. We did not make a lot of money from these versions, but we did make a lot of friends. Eventually, we were given a lot of help from various hardware companies to promote our product, primarily because they had so few products to promote.

None of these incompatible computers sold very well. The best-selling incompatible machine was the DEC Rainbow, which had the advantage of either working as a terminal for a DEC computer or running MS/DOS or CP/M. Even with this and other technical advantages and the strength of DEC behind it, the computer never had a chance. Customers didn't want to wait around for their favorite software to be available on incompatibles, and software companies quickly tired of the porting. Soon, the hardware companies began to copy IBM's machine exactly, producing what were called "clones." The clones were able to run software made for the IBM PC, and the huge fees for porting software vanished.

At first we sold most of our software to dealers rather than to distributors. A dealer to us was any company that sold its products directly to end users—that is, the people who actually used the products. A distributor was a company that sold products only to dealers. We sold through dealers because we couldn't find any distributors willing to carry our product, even though we offered them an attractive discount. The large distributors like Softsel and Micro D sent rejection letters telling us they already had plenty of word processors.

Our first dealer to order more than one or two copies at a time was 47th Street Photo: They were a perfect account—they ordered in quantities of ten or twenty and paid COD. When I offered to give them thirty days to pay, they declined the credit. Louis Schwartz, the man I dealt with, said he knew we were small and needed the money. At the time, we knew nothing about 47th Street Photo, except that they were a great account in the New York City area. Later, we learned that they were disliked by almost all of our other dealers because of their very low prices. Despite the pleas that later came from these dealers, I could never agree to cut off 47th Street. Their help in those early months had been far too valuable.

ComputerLand gave us our first big break when they picked us up in the spring of 1983. They were the largest chain of retail computer stores and the most important part of IBM's dealer network. A decision by Computer-Land's corporate headquarters to sell a product was an important seal of approval. In addition to the industry-wide recognition that came with their endorsement, the various ComputerLand stores were much more likely to sell a recommended product over an unrecommended one.

At the time, ComputerLand would accept any product for review, as long as the software vendor sent in nine free copies. Eight of these were sent to the eight Compu-terLand stores that composed the evaluation committee, and one copy stayed at CL headquarters. The stores on the committee were kept secret, so vendors couldn't lobby directly with committee members for approval. The committee met periodically by telephone to discuss the merits of each product and to decide which products the chain would carry. Around the first of the year, we submitted nine copies of WordPerfect and waited impatiently for the verdict.

Although I'm not sure we knew it at the time, the Baltimore ComputerLand store was on the committee and liked our product a lot. Will Fastie, who lived near the Baltimore store and worked for General Instrument, used our DG version. He also wrote a column devoted to the IBM PC for the magazine *Creative Computing*. Because he liked our DG version, he encouraged his friends at the Baltimore ComputerLand to try the PC version, and they became enthusiastic supporters.

The ComputerLand of Fox River in Oshkosh, Wisconsin, was the only other committee member to recommend our product, and its recommendation came almost by accident. I had traveled to Wisconsin at the request of Kimberly-Clark (the Kleenex company), which was in the middle of a word-processing evaluation and was soliciting demonstrations from different vendors. I arrived in Wisconsin on the afternoon before my appointment and called on computer stores to fill up my afternoon. I happened to stop at the ComputerLand of Fox River, and having nothing better to do, I spent a few hours looking at our competitors' products while waiting to talk with the store's owners, John and Carol Teska. At the end of the day, I finally had an opportunity to tell them about WordPerfect's great features and mentioned my visit to Kimberly-Clark. John told me KC was his client, and I invited him to the demonstration.

Luckily, the ComputerLand evaluation committee was meeting the evening after my appointment with Kimberly-Clark, and because he had seen KC's positive reaction, John recommended it to the committee. We had only two committee stores out of eight that wanted to carry our product, but two was enough.

Getting picked up by the chain was only half the battle; we still had to convince the rest of the stores to sell WordPerfect. We asked two college kids, Scott Worthington and John Lee, to take some time off from school to visit ComputerLand stores across the country. Scott went east and John went west, and they spent the next nine months collecting Holiday Inn "frequent-sleeper" points. They went from city to city, dropping off a dem-

onstration copy at each store and showing WordPerfect
to as many salespeople as they could.

Our smartest marketing move that year was to offer
ComputerLand employees the chance to buy one copy of
WordPerfect for ten dollars if they would take a simple
test. WordStar was so popular at the time that it was
almost impossible to get salespeople to try any other
word processor. Although most of them were WordStar
fanatics through and through, the ten dollar offer was
too good for many to pass up. The questions on the test
were very easy. We asked things such as: "Does WordPerfect or WordStar have the largest dictionary?" The correct answer to every question was "WordPerfect," but the
salesperson had to do some comparisons to verify the
answers. Quite a few salespeople started using WordPerfect at home as a result.

By the time ComputerLand held its annual owners'
conference that summer, we were the chain's second best-
selling word processor. Although we were second, we still
trailed far behind WordStar. During the conference at the
Fairmont Hotel in San Francisco, we booked a suite and
invited the owners to drop by. Only six people came, and
only two actually came into our suite. We didn't understand that the hospitality suites were for having fun, not
for doing business, and our shrimp and egg rolls couldn't
compete with the mixed drinks served in other suites.
Those of us from SSI sat all alone, eating our expensive
shrimp in our expensive suite until we were sick.

The next day of the conference went much better. We
had a small booth at the vendor fair, which was a small
trade show where store owners and managers could
wander around, talk to vendors, and watch demonstrations. As people walked by, we literally grabbed them
and dragged them into our booth. We were too eager and
naive to be shy or to believe we might have been bothering anybody.

Microsoft was about to release its word processor,
Word, which we saw for the first time at the conference.

We had been a little worried about the product, because we knew the company had the resources to do a good job. One look at Word, however, erased all our worries. The product was no more innovative than its name. Microsoft had designed Word along the lines of its spreadsheet, Multiplan. It was clumsy to use and came with no new or interesting features. You could tell the Microsoft programmers had not talked to many secretaries while developing their product. It would take Microsoft a little more work before they would be a significant factor in the word-processing market.

In mid-1983, Terry Brown (the documentation writer we'd hired in 1981) and I went to Syntopican, a trade show for word-processing department managers. At the time, almost all word processing was done by a company's word-processing department. The manager of the department, usually a woman, commanded a lot of power and influence inside her company, because she decided whose work would get finished first. When the managers met at Syntopican, they were treated like queens and kings by the dedicated-word-processor computer vendors. IBM, CPT, Wang, Dictaphone, DEC, Xerox, and NBI were just a few of the companies spending millions of dollars trying to win their favor. As Terry and I toured the trade show, we were amazed to find so many companies spending so much money on a dying industry. The dedicated word processor was quickly giving way to the personal computer, but not many people at Syntopican seemed to see it coming. The managers had trouble believing that executives would soon be typing their own letters and that, within three or four years, their jobs would disappear.

Although we were not doing as well as Lotus, our sales were growing steadily each quarter. After doing $427,000 for the first quarter, we reached $645,000 in the second, and $843,000 in the third. In September, we were actually mentioned as a best-seller in *Softalk*, a trade magazine which has since gone out of business. We were

twenty-second on their list of top-selling software products, which made us the fifth word processor, behind
WordStar, Word Plus, MultiMate, and PFS:Write. Although ComputerLand's list wasn't published, we discovered we were twelfth on their hot list—the second
best-selling word processor in their stores.

As sales grew, we were hiring as many people as our
budget would allow. We had no formal method for advertising our job openings, so everyone we hired was
either a friend, a neighbor, a relative, a passerby, or a
student in one of Alan's classes. Doug Lloyd, for example, was a salesman from IBM's Salt Lake office who
dropped by to see if we needed a large computer. We
didn't buy a computer, but we did offer him a job. Doug
became our chief salesperson for large accounts.

Bruce hired my brother André, though he didn't let
me know until after he'd done it. He knew Dan and I
needed some help and that I was reluctant to hire more
people for marketing. Although I was happy to see my
brother get out of the drapery business, I was depressed
about sharing my duties with someone else. I was going
through the same kind of discouragement I would watch
others experience over the years. As an organization adds
people, some responsibilities must be taken away from
the older employees and given to the newer ones. It is a
process which is usually painful but necessary, if everyone in a company is to have a meaningful job. André's
job was to keep track of our dealers and attempt to sell
our products to distributors.

We increased our customer support department to
four people. Until then, support calls were unofficially
answered by everyone in the company. This method
worked fairly well for the Data General support because
we didn't get very many calls. It did not work well for
the PC product, however.

If I remember correctly, our toll-free support was
somewhat of an accident, rather than a conscious marketing strategy. When we first released WordPerfect, we

had a toll-free number for orders, and a regular number for our other calls. Our customers outsmarted us, however; most used the free number whenever they needed help. To keep the order lines clear for orders, we added a toll-free number for support. On two or three occasions during 1984 and 1985, we considered dropping the toll-free support to save money, but each time, we convinced ourselves that the service was worth the cost. After a few years, we had received so much good press for the service that it was impossible to curtail it. The service was very consistent with our "good guys in the white hats" image.

We were also hiring programmers. While it may not seem logical, once a product goes out the door, a software developer always needs to add more programmers to the project. Releasing a product is a lot like having an older child move out of the house and having a new baby move in. The product that ships, like the child who moves out, still has problems and needs some attention, and the new version, like a new baby, also demands a lot of attention. Producing a better version inevitably means a bigger and more complex program, which many times requires even more work than the first version. Fixing bugs is only a part of the maintenance required to support software once it ships. As new printers, monitors, graphics cards, keyboards, and hard drives are introduced, more programming work is necessary to support these new peripherals—just about anything that plugs into the periphery or any other part of a computer is called a peripheral—and keep a product up-to-date.

In addition to meeting programming needs for our existing products, we also wanted more programmers for new products. When we first released WordPerfect 2.0, many large corporations told us they weren't interested in our word processor unless we had a complete family of products. As it turned out, this excuse quickly disappeared with the success of 1-2-3, because practically every large company bought the Lotus spreadsheet, even though it was the only product the company offered. With this excuse eliminated and with companies looking for the best product in each category, it would have been logical for us to abandon the family-of-products strategy, but we didn't. Much like the mountain climber who climbed the mountain because it was there, we were intent on writing a new software product whenever we had the opportunity.

Dave Moon, another of Alan's bright students, headed up a project to develop a spreadsheet, which we first called MathPlan and later PlanPerfect. Lew Bastian, Bruce's oldest brother, came from IBM to write a legal-time-and-billing system called SSI*Legal and a version of the computer language FORTH. Eventually, he would expand the scope of his work and produce a database called SSI*Data, later called DataPerfect. We were also working on a communications program called TranSSIt.

In spite of all these other projects, most of the programmers were working on WordPerfect 3.0. There were a number of new features, but the most important improvement was the new printer code. In the 2.2x versions (2.2x stands for 2.20, 2.21, and 2.23), we treated all printers except the Diablo and Epson printers as if they were "dumb" printers. A dumb printer is one that can't do anything except print a standard set of characters (a character is a letter, a number, or a symbol on the keyboard) in a fixed pitch (fixed pitch characters all have the same width, while proportionally spaced characters can vary in width). A dumb printer cannot print proportionally spaced characters or different fonts, or do any of the more attractive things printers with smarts can do. If you had a smart printer that was not one of the two we supported, you could not use all your printer's features with WordPerfect 2.2x. Even with a Diablo printer, which had our best support, you could not print proportionally spaced text.

Our less-than-great printer support was a big drawback, because it was important to have a computer document look like it was professionally typewritten. For some reason, the early computer users wanted to hide the fact that a computer was doing much of the work. It would take a couple of years before people considered using a computer as a status symbol. The professional typewritten look was called "letter quality" in the industry, and one of our goals for WordPerfect 3.0 was for it to be able to print a letter that looked as good as one typed on an IBM Executive typewriter.

Our biggest problem supporting the "smarts" in many printers was that all of our printer instructions were hard-coded into WordPerfect. Having hard-coded printer instructions meant that they were written inside the WordPerfect program, which meant that whenever we wanted to add a new printer, we had to add more code to WordPerfect. Since there were hundreds of printers on the market, adding code for each of them would have made the program far too big, not to mention the nightmare it would have been to release a new version of WordPerfect every time we added another printer's instructions.

The solution was to put the printer instructions in "tables" outside the program. A table is nothing more than a list of values. A box score in the sports section of the newspaper is a table. In a box score for a basketball game, for example, each player's name is listed with values for minutes played, points scored, rebounds, turnovers, etc. In a printer table, the printer features are listed along with the instructions that are sent to the printer for each feature. A printer table held the instructions for things like turning bold on, turning bold off, or turning underlining on. For version 3.0 of WordPerfect, the printer code was entirely rewritten to use look-up tables for all printer instructions.

As a result of the change, our biggest weakness in 2.2x became our biggest strength in 3.0. We bought and borrowed all kinds of printers, and by the time we released 3.0, we supported more than fifty of them. Within a year after the release, we supported about two-hundred printers, more than any other word processor. We could also add support for new printers faster than our competition. We even included a special program that let users make their own tables or drivers for printers our software didn't support. The program could also be used to make changes to our printer definitions, should a user want to improve on our work.

The only disadvantage to the table-driven method was that printing was a little slower. Unfortunately, we underestimated how vocal and angry a few of our customers would get because of the printing slowdown. We quickly learned that, no matter how many improvements we made to a new version, if we took something away, we would have many unhappy customers. Some customers demanded a partial refund for the printing delays; however, I don't think we gave them any money back.

In the fall, we introduced the new version at COMDEX. COMDEX, which is short for COMputer Dealer EXposition, was the biggest computer trade show in the United States. It was expensive, noisy, crowded, tiring, and absolutely essential for almost everyone in the computer industry. The fall version of COMDEX was always held in Las Vegas, which was fitting because a lot of companies spent their last dollars to get there, gambling that they could find enough interest in their products to stay in business a little longer. Ours was the smallest space you could rent, a ten-by-ten-foot booth located at the far end of the convention hall, facing the back wall. The largest booth spaces were sometimes as large as ten-thousand square feet or more.

In addition to paying for booth space, companies had to pay for the booths themselves. A booth could easily cost $100,000, and a few companies spent more than $1,000,000 on their booths. Once a booth was paid for, a company had to pay shipping charges to send it to and from the show, as well as set-up charges, charges

to run power to the booth and put computers in the
booth, and the costs of sending employees, models, and
actors to the show to work the booth. (We didn't use
models, because we were all so good looking.)

Our first booth was not very extravagant. Dan was in
charge, and he managed to cram four computers and six
workers into our small area. Those of us who worked the
show dragged as many people as we could into the booth
for a demonstration. Though our booth was minuscule
compared to Micropro's (the WordStar company), we
were proud of ourselves nonetheless. Just making it
there and getting the booth set up seemed like a great
accomplishment.

One man who came by our booth was from one of
the Big Three automakers. He offered me $250,000 for a
site license to run WordPerfect on all their Victor 9000
machines. That was a lot of money, but I was very idealistic and turned him down. Even though our company
had little money in savings, I did not want to sell them
a license to run WP on all their current and future Victor
machines for a one-time fee: I wanted us to make a little
money on each new machine they brought into their
company. (Later, the auto company dropped the Victor
9000 and replaced all their machines with IBM PCs. We
could have taken their money for the Victor software and
then sold them new copies for the IBM PC.)

We were all a little in awe of companies like Micropro. They had a very large, beautiful booth and what
seemed like thousands of people jamming into it to look
at their products. At the time, I don't think any of us ever
dreamed we would out do them. We were a little frustrated because we knew we had a better product, but we
didn't know how to use this advantage to overtake Word-
Star. Micropro was outselling us by about twenty to one.

With only $60,000 of savings in the bank as a war
chest, we didn't have the money to fight Micropro aggressively. Unless we changed our minds about going
into debt or selling off part of the company, we had to

be content to continue on our course, growing when we had the money. This was probably a good thing because we were not yet smart enough to spend a lot of money wisely. We were no longer like innocent little children, but we were still only beginning to learn about things such as distribution strategies, product branding, product life cycles, and test marketing. Our advertising was still homemade, and our public relations was not very good; we still didn't know how to make friends with the press.

In spite of our frustration and our inexperience, we were happy to finish 1983 with $3.5 million in sales, up from about $1 million in 1982. Because about half of the sales came in the last quarter, after the release of version 3.0, we were confident that we could at least double sales again in 1984. We were barely coping with the problems that came with the sales increases, but we were surviving. We were starting to get favorable reports in the press. The dealer survey in the November issue of *Softalk* announced that WordPerfect had been the best-selling word processor in October. While we knew this wasn't true, it did show that there were at least a few dealers who liked our product. More importantly, our customers loved us and were saying good things about us to their friends.

# 5

# GROWTH SPURT

---

As 3.0's sales took off, the company started to feel like a fast-moving train, running totally out of control. We couldn't stop it, we didn't know how to steer it, and we were not sure where we were headed. All we could do was hold on and hope for the best.

We were a group of friends, relatives, and neighbors, all working hard and trying our best, but lacking any formal structure to our organization. Meetings were held whenever two or more people happened to pass in the hallway. We lacked any official methods for considering ideas or making decisions. If someone came up with an idea, we usually gave it a try—our only constraint on experimentation was the amount of cash we had in the bank. If we could afford it, we tried it.

Alan liked to tell the press that our success was a result of hiring good people and letting them do a good job. His analysis always discouraged me, because I liked to think the leadership and management of the board was primarily responsible for our success. Looking back, Alan's opinion was probably closer to the truth. The board exercised enough control to keep the company profitable, but we let people do what they wanted to do most of the time.

The background we shared helped us hold things together. Most of us came from Utah or were somehow connected to the state through BYU or the Mormon church. Many of our great-grandparents were pioneers who had come west long before Utah was granted statehood. Most of them arrived with little money and few possessions after suffering religious persecution. Our grandparents and parents, especially those who stayed in Utah, generally had a tough time making a living. Utah was not a rich state and was known for its low wages.

As children, we were taught that hard work and self-reliance were virtues and that debt should be avoided like the plague. We generally grew up in homes of modest means and were not accustomed to luxury or extravagance. Most of us didn't drink or smoke. We expected to work long hours for few rewards. Honest, cheerful, and happy to have our jobs, we were a personnel manager's dream come true.

We loved running our own company. Most businesses that came to Utah did so because of our low labor costs, and most chose to import their own management teams. The opportunity we had to make our own decisions and control the nature and culture of our company was unusual. We enjoyed our independence, and that was an extra incentive for everyone to make sure we continued to be profitable.

Turning a profit in 1984 was not very difficult, although if the reviews of WP 3.0 had been bad, we might have had a tougher time. Fortunately, the one that mattered most, the *InfoWorld* review, was merely lukewarm and not bad enough to hurt us. Although our overall score was disappointing and a little puzzling, the author of the review wrote some very complimentary things about our product. Most of the reviews in the other trade publications were much more positive. We were now getting enough attention from the industry press that government agencies and large corporations were including WordPerfect in many of their evaluations.

Sales jumped to more than $2 million for the first quarter of 1984. We were surprised and excited to be doing so well, but we had trouble believing sales would stay at such a high level. We kept our expenses down to $1 million a quarter in case the high sales proved to be an aberration.

This huge growth in sales, however, meant we needed more people, more office space, more computers, and more telephones. We probably also needed a little more structure to our organization, but we didn't know what to do at the time. Our informal, all-for-one-and-one-for-all, family-type of company had worked well with twenty-five employees, but was showing signs of breaking down now that we had more than fifty. Many things were happening, and at times, no one seemed to know why. We had trouble keeping everyone up-to-date and working together. We had to keep adding more people for development, marketing, customer support, manufacturing, and order-taking, but unfortunately, we gave them almost no training and little supervision. Each department was its own little empire, with its own policies and procedures.

We dealt with the changes using a strategy I called "crisis growth." Rather than anticipating and planning for problems, we solved them as they came up. This strategy was forced upon us, because although we were showing a good profit, we were growing so quickly that we never seemed to have enough money to pay for a permanent solution. We never had enough money to build or lease a building that would hold the entire company, so we leased space around Orem as we needed it. We never seemed to be able to hire enough customer support operators to handle all the calls, so we did the best we could with the resources we had. It seemed like we needed a bigger telephone switch, more telephone lines, better computers, and more office space every month.

Perhaps if we had gone public or raised money in some other way, we could have done a more professional job of handling the growth. At the time, however, we were more concerned with keeping our independence. We were happy to take things one day at a time. I am not sure where we got the confidence to think we could do this forever, but the longer we did it successfully, the less we worried about the future.

There were some benefits to this crisis growth strategy. It is always dangerous to spend money in anticipation of growth. A company that does runs the risk of having too many employees, too much equipment, and too few sales to cover its costs. Wang is a good example. They planned on getting bigger and bigger, so they built large, beautiful buildings to hold all the people they would need to hire. When their business slowed down, they were left with hundreds of thousands of square feet of empty office space.

By growing only at the very last minute, we never ran out of money. Sometimes our customers would get a busy signal, sometimes employees would have to share offices, and sometimes we all had to work a little harder to keep up, but we rarely had to lay anyone off and we never had to borrow any money.

Our most difficult crisis at the time was maintaining good communications inside the company. There were, of course, informal lines of communication, but a friend-to-friend network of gossip and rumors was not the ideal way to get information distributed. Our solution was not perfect, but it helped. Alan and I used our lunch hours to run our areas of the company, setting up a very complicated schedule so we could eat with the different department heads on a regular basis. We brought the marketing and development departments

together at a large luncheon every Monday, and we met
with smaller groups from Tuesday through Friday. That
way, we found out what each of the groups was doing
and offered advice as we ate. If problems arose between
different groups, we would put them together at a luncheon to sort things out. Gaining weight almost became
a part of our job descriptions.

We learned a lot about the dynamics of communicating around a dining table. We learned that a luncheon
of more than eight people was generally unproductive,
because it led to multiple conversations that were usually off the subject. Six seemed to be the best number for
getting work done. A round table was better than a rectangular one. If a rectangular table was the only option,
it was always better to sit in one of the middle seats if
you wanted to be involved in the discussions.

As we met with the different groups and began to
understand more of what was happening inside the company, we discovered how very little control we had.
Many in the company had grown accustomed to doing
whatever they wanted and were having trouble listening
to suggestions and keeping the board up-to-date on their
work. Because the company was doing so well, it was
hard to make big changes. We started to exert a measure
of control by creating a budgeting process. If we liked
what we heard at lunch, we funded the efforts. If we
didn't like what we heard, we limited spending or
hiring.

Our management-by-luncheon system did not help
international business, however, which was Bruce's part
of the organization. He spent much of his time traveling
in Europe and other parts of the world and did not eat
with us very often. We had very little contact with the
people he hired, so our international business was isolated from our domestic business. Communication between the two was always a problem.

Our increasing sales and good reviews were finally
bringing calls from distributors. Instead of sending re-

jection letters, most were asking us to sign distribution agreements. Sears was the only exception. They took the time to send us a second rejection letter.

Deciding to use distributors was not easy. One consideration was money. Our dealers received a 50 percent discount on the list price of our products. Distributors told us they needed at least a 65 percent discount to make a profit, and the $75 difference seemed like a lot. A second consideration was the additional discounting that was bound to occur with distributors. At the time, the neighborhood computer dealer was the software vendor's most important sales channel. If we wanted the dealers' loyalty, we were expected to keep our product out of the hands of mail-order companies. The dealers wanted to charge a higher price and did not want to have to compete with the discounters.

We tried our best to comply with the dealers' demands, but it wasn't easy. Although we kept WordPerfect out of the hands of reputable mail-order companies by refusing to sell to them, other, less-reputable mail-order companies were selling the product. Ironically, they were buying it from a few of the dealers we were trying to protect. As soon as we could find the dealers who were selling to mail-order companies, we cut them off. However, as quickly as we stopped selling to one misbehaving dealer, another would start up. No matter how hard we tried, every month a few ads appeared offering WordPerfect at a discount.

We knew that if we used distributors, the situation would only get worse. Once a distributor has a product, it's available everywhere, because they will sell to almost anyone with a sales-tax number and a good story. Selling through distributors meant no longer trying to eliminate the discounters. In the years to come, we learned to listen politely and sympathetically to the dealers' pleas for help, but we never found a practical and legal way to protect them.

There were advantages to having distributors which

outweighed these other considerations. Because dealers
carry hundreds of items in a store, it is inconvenient and
impractical for them to order all those items directly
from each manufacturer: They needed good distributors
who could deliver many products quickly. Distributors
helped us out, because it was much easier for us to service a few of them than it was to service many thousands
of dealers. And the customers—the people who actually
bought and used WordPerfect—benefited. As soon as distributors started carrying WordPerfect, the dealer price
for it went down and the competition among the dealers
increased. The street price, or the price customers paid
if they shopped around, ended up dropping below $300
for our $495 piece of software.

When we started to sign up distributors, we made the
mistake of agreeing to two or three of their contracts
before we understood how much these agreements fa-
vored them. After we realized our error, we had them
sign an agreement more to our liking. WordPerfect was
selling well enough now that we could get away with
drafting and enforcing our own agreements.

Once we started signing up distributors, we didn't
seem to know how to stop. Before we realized that there
was such a thing as being "overdistributed," we had almost twenty distributors. Five or six would have been
more than enough to ensure that our products were com-
petitively priced. Unfortunately, it would take us years
to get rid of the excess.

In April, Doug Lloyd was given approval to start a
summer "rep" program. ("Rep" was short for "marketing representative.") By now, the two college students,
Scott and John, were home from their travels around the
country, and Doug, well versed in IBM's sales strategies,
wanted to try his hand at putting together a new outside
sales force. We gave him permission to hire ten or twelve
people for the summer.

We posted the job opportunities on a bulletin board
at BYU's placement office. Doug watched as the prospec-

tive salespeople arrived, interviewing those he thought looked good, and letting Scott interview those he didn't. I think he was looking for people who had that IBM look—at least six feet tall, good hair, nice clothes, and an energetic walk. Doug hired about ten men and one woman, all good-looking, all in their early twenties, and all with their own cars. Most had been on missions for the Mormon church as well.

The training the reps received was minimal. I asked Doug to give them at least twenty-seven hours of instruction, and that was all they got. During the last two weeks of the semester, they each spent about sixteen hours on the computer to learn WordPerfect, a few hours in the classroom to learn a sales pitch, and four hours in customer support to listen in on support calls. With this small amount of training and a trunk full of demonstration copies of WordPerfect, we sent them on their way.

We were lucky to have started the program when the dealers still had time to talk to salespeople. Some would even take the reps under their wing and show them how to use a hard disk (the reps had only learned how to use a two-floppy disk drive system) and give a good demonstration. In spite of the limited training and lack of support from the home office, most of the reps did a very good job. About half went back to school in the fall, but the other half stayed out in the field to work for us full-time.

Development work on the next version of WordPerfect was moving ahead very slowly. Our biggest distraction was trying to find a way to stop people from stealing our software. Back then, Lotus 1-2-3 was copy-protected and was bringing in more money than any other application. A lot of our employees thought our sales would improve considerably if we also used copy-protection. Bruce felt copy-protection was an absolute requirement if we were to sell our software in Europe successfully, since a very large percentage of Europeans were pirating software. Trade publications estimated that at least 50 percent of the software used in the United States was pirated. Europeans were thought to be pirating as much as 75 percent of their copies. In countries like Spain and Italy, the percentage of stolen copies was believed to be even higher.

One option would be to pay another company for protection. Some companies sold tiny devices for about $10 that had to be plugged into the back of the computer for a software product to work. Other companies sold special, modified disks, called "key disks," which had to stay in the disk drive for a program to work. Royalties for key disks were about $2 to $5 per copy.

We wanted to avoid paying royalties, so we began developing our own key disk type of copy-protection. During the first half of 1984, the developers came up with different ways to protect against the copying, but they were never completely satisfied that their schemes were unbreakable. We were rapidly coming to the conclusion that developing an inexpensive, unbreakable protection scheme was an impossible task. Meanwhile, software customers were coming to the conclusion that any protection was too much of an inconvenience.

Our other products were also taking resources away from WordPerfect. IBM had announced the IBM PC jr, so in addition to the products we had begun, we were developing a word processor and a spreadsheet for this new machine. We believed that we had to broaden our product line to compete. We were determined that 1984 would "mark the end of the one-product company, and the emergence of SSI as a significant software company with many products for IBM small computers." (This quotation was taken from our 1984 business plan.)

In retrospect, we should have used more of our resources to improve WordPerfect, but we were preoccupied with offering a family of products, and shedding our one-product-company label. There was a common belief in the industry that was regularly reported in the trade press: A one-product company had to diversify to be successful.

Even our bankers and accountants were asking us if we could survive long term without diversifying.

Like almost every other software company, we were caught up in the rage to have a complete suite of applications, all with a similar brand name. Software Publishing had PFS:Write and PFS:File. Micropro had WordStar, CalcStar, and DataStar. The PerfectWriter people also had PerfectCalc. A company formed by a few Micropro exiles had WriteIt and CalcIt and plans for DataIt and DrawIt. Of course, none of these product families were successful, but that didn't stop any of us from trying.

Sometime in the late spring or early summer we realized we were wasting valuable time and that we needed to get a good, new version of WordPerfect ready for the fall. The obvious name for the new version was WordPerfect 4.0. The number represented a perfect grade point average in school and described the type of product we wanted to release. Although we didn't have time to add in a lot of new features, we did have the time and the resources to improve its cosmetics.

Alan finally agreed that the old keyboard template had to go. It had covered the ten function keys on the keyboard's left side as well as the number keys across the top. It looked like an "L" tipped over. I liked to call it the "gallows" template, both because it seemed to be killing sales and because it resembled the figure you draw to start the game Hangman. It did not stay on the keyboard well and did not fit many of the new clones' keyboards. By moving all the features to the ten function keys, we could create a less-complicated template that would fit on more keyboards.

We spent a lot of time and money on the 4.0 manual, using better paper, more color, and adding a tutorial with exercises. We also added a nicer-looking jacket to the outside of the package. These enhancements gave the impression that 4.0 itself was a much improved program, even though the software hadn't changed much. There were some new features. Installation was simpler, the dictionary was bigger, a block was now highlighted on the screen, endnotes were added, and error-handling was better (WP could now recover from many DOS errors that used to make it crash). But there were not nearly as many new features as there had been in 3.0.

Until the last minute, we planned to include a simple, key disk copy-protection for 4.0, which required users to insert a WordPerfect disk each time they started the program. I personally did not enjoy the procedure and begged Alan to use it himself before we shipped. (He had been using nonprotected software on his own machine to save time when switching back and forth between P-Edit and WordPerfect.) After about fifteen minutes of using the protected software, Alan told the developers to drop the protection. It was so close to the release that we didn't have time to remove the key symbol, which signified a copy-protected disk, from the labels.

Dropping the copy-protection was a good decision. Although we would still copy-protect some of our software in Europe, it just wasn't a good idea in the United States. Here, many businesses weren't willing to live with the inconvenience of copy-protection. Even 1-2-3 would eventually drop it. It was simply not fair to make the honest, paying customers put up with an inconvenience that had been made necessary by the dishonest ones. In the end, what was good for the legal customers was also good for our bottom line.

We shipped 4.0 a couple of weeks before COMDEX to be ready for the year-end selling season. There was a feeling of great excitement around the company; version 4.0 symbolized "A" work, and we were proud of our efforts. It seemed as if all our employees had been involved in making the product a success.

Bruce was adamant that we spend every dime we had on the 4.0 roll-out. He wanted no less than $100,000 budgeted for advertising. This seemed like an enormous amount, since we usually budgeted only $15,000 a month for advertising.

Our booth at COMDEX was six times the size of the previous year's booth. We put a stage in the booth and hired a trade show company from Chicago to do a presentation. Their production included professional actors, singing, and dancing. We did not want to look like a technical software house from some remote spot in the Rocky Mountains; we wanted to look like a software publisher with exciting products and new ideas.

During our evenings at COMDEX, a few of us, including a couple of programmers, met to share stories and impressions from the show. Some were discouraged by our image compared to that of the other large companies and complained about how difficult it was to improve it without a lot of money. We were, however, already well on the way to enhancing our reputation. In addition to our improved product and our professional presentation at COMDEX, Dan was using an advertising agency. At their suggestion, we had a new logo, new packaging on the way, a new ad campaign, and a new name. The new name, SSI Software, didn't make a lot of sense—Satellite Software International Software?—but it looked good in the ads. We no longer looked like amateurs. We had improved to at least a semiprofessional level overall, and were beginning to get things right.

Some of our employees nonetheless felt that the image we projected would hinder our growth. We had a young, bright, cheerful, clean-scrubbed, naive kind of look, and as a result many in the industry, including our competitors, did not take us seriously. Although we didn't appear as sophisticated and cosmopolitan as some would have liked, I had trouble believing we should try to assume an image that didn't fit us very well. I didn't think it was fair to complain about the truth, any more than it was fair to complain that a bunny rabbit had floppy ears and a tail. However it was fair to expect that we should do our work expertly.

Until COMDEX of 1984, my hope was to one day
capture 35 percent of the word-processing market. We
had outsold a lot of other products—Select, Benchmark,
Palantir, Peachtext, Volkswriter, and EasyWriter—but
Micropro's WordStar seemed impassable. WordStar had
no less than 60 percent of the market, and their dealers
and customers were very loyal. All Micropro had to do
was to keep offering improved versions of WordStar to
maintain their number-one position.

Unfortunately for Micropro, the one thing they
could not do very easily was update their product. After
their luck in getting the CP/M version of WordStar running on the PC, they couldn't seem to get an updated
version out the door. They decided instead to produce an
entirely new product, one which was easier to maintain
and improve than the original version.

The new WordStar, introduced at COMDEX as
WordStar 2000, was entirely different from the old product. Fortunately for us, Micropro intentionally attempted to replace their market leader with a product that was
bigger and slower and used a different interface. Although it wasn't obvious at the time, the product was
doomed from the start. In spite of all the product hype
and the size and beauty of the Micropro booth and presentation, it didn't stand a chance.

Micropro did more for us at that show than we could
ever have done for ourselves. They convinced their customers that the old WordStar was not very good and that
they needed to look for something better. What Micropro
didn't realize was that not only would their customers
take a look at WordStar 2000, they would also look at
WordPerfect 4.0.

We finished the year with sales of a little more than
$9 million, which made us the third best-selling word
processor, behind WordStar ($67 million) and Multi-
mate ($20 million). Even though our profits for the year
were slightly more than $1 million after taxes, we had

very little cash. Every dollar we made was going back into the company or toward the promotion of 4.0.

Our hopes to have many successful products by the end of the year were not realized. The IBM PC jr was failing, as were the products we made for it, and none of our other products was selling very well. Most disappointing of all were the prospects for SSI*Data. It had come out just before COMDEX, and the *InfoWorld* review appeared in their Christmas Eve edition. The review was much worse than bad. We received only a one-disk rating, the worst possible. Their conclusion was: "This one needs work before you should consider purchasing it." The failure was particularly disappointing to me, because for a year and a half I had spent a lot of time working on the product.

Lew Bastian, older brother to Bruce and my wife and the sole programmer of the original SSI*Data, remained in Tucson after leaving IBM. For most of the month he worked on his software project at home, and for one week each month he would come up to Utah to visit the SSI offices. During these visits, he would stay with me and my family.

My kids liked having their uncle around because he would pick them up and run around the room so they could pretend they were Superman or Superwoman. My wife loved her oldest brother, but his week-long visits were not very much fun for her. I spent every evening with Lew learning about his legal-time-and-billing system and watching him write his program in FORTH (I was, as I said, past being merely a workaholic). One evening, we were downstairs talking about his program, when we came up with this great idea for a database. It was another "Ah hah!" type experience, and it was exciting to visualize the product and think about how great it would be to use.

I was so convinced that what we envisioned was good that I spent all my spare time working on it. Once Lew had a prototype working, I started showing it off to the press, and one magazine, *PC World,* did a major story about it in their February 1984 issue. Through spring and summer, I wrote the manual, and in the early fall, I did the alpha testing all by myself and organized the beta testing. I wanted so much to see the product come to life as we had originally designed it that I wouldn't let anyone help me.

So convinced was I of its success that the very negative review in *InfoWorld* was a complete surprise. The reviewer disliked the manual and was disappointed by all the bugs. Though I hated to admit it, what he said was true. The failure of SSI*Data taught me two painful lessons: Ideas should be shared so others can improve on them; and no one, including myself, is infallible.

Lew would struggle to improve SSI*Data year after year. Eventually, we changed the name to DataPerfect and many customers bought it, but the reviews never got much better. The product sold well enough to finance its development, but it never made us a significant amount of money.

Even with the failures, our SSI train—now our SSI Software train—was getting bigger and rolling down the tracks even faster. Sales for WordPerfect overshadowed all our other mistakes. No matter what we did wrong, no matter how we misused our resources, WordPerfect for DOS provided more than enough money to keep us out of trouble and make us look good.

To our credit, we did have our share of successes. Our toll-free customer support was already a well-recognized marketing asset. Unlike Micropro, who referred their customers to dealers for assistance, we wanted to help our customers personally. We wanted to hear their complaints and their suggestions.

Perhaps our image was a little too nice for some, but in a year we had almost tripled sales and grown from forty-seven employees to eighty-four employees. We had our share of problems, but we were all going the extra mile and learning from our mistakes.

# 6

# GROWING PAINS

---

We told the world in our new, professional ad campaign that WordPerfect 4.0 was the most perfect Word-Perfect ever, and the product was worthy of the hype. It was fast, reliable, and significantly better than our competition. Now all we had to do was convince the software buyers of the world that we were right.

This was not an easy job, because word-processor users were almost fanatic about their favorite products. For most people, switching from one product to another was almost unthinkable. Many found WordStar especially hard to learn and master, and fans of the product defended it with an irrational fervor. Their loyalty was similar to that of a mother who has given birth to a very ugly baby. It was almost impossible to get expert Word-Star users to admit the program had any flaws.

The die-hard WordStar users naturally recommended it to friends and coworkers, and this very vocal group represented our biggest obstacle convincing new customers to buy our product. Luckily, Micropro made our job easy by attempting to replace WordStar with WordStar 2000. They tried to fix all the problems in the original WordStar, and rather than making their loyalists happy, they alienated them. Their strongest supporters had bonded to the program's quirks and problems and had come to believe that the difficulties were desirable. Worst of all, WordStar 2000 was very slow compared to the old WordStar. Even a mother couldn't have loved it.

As far as I can remember, only one reviewer, Ronni Marshak, liked WordStar 2000, but despite her comment that it had "soundly thrashed" WordPerfect 4.0, Micropro's sales headed downward. After reaching a high of $67 million in 1984, they declined to $43 million in 1985. Micropro would eventually realize its mistake and try to push the original WordStar, but its sales figures would never improve.

The *InfoWorld* review of WordPerfect 3.0 in 1985 had been somewhat schizophrenic, extending compliments while giving us a less than positive overall rating. The 4.0 review, however, had only one personality—it was positive in the extreme. The final sentence of the review read, "We believe WordPerfect 4.0 represents a new standard of excellence for microcomputer word processors." They gave us a perfect rating, with a grade of excellent in every category.

The *InfoWorld* rating was worth millions of dollars to us. The perfect score became the theme for all our advertising. We reprinted the review and sent copies everywhere. When we called on customers, we made sure they saw copies of it. When we visited our dealers, we made sure they had plenty of copies to hand out. We had been given a great endorsement by the most influential computer publication, and we did our best to make the most of it.

Our January sales topped $1 million—our first million-dollar month—and Bruce and Alan took the whole company out to lunch to celebrate. Over the course of the year, sales would only get better. Bruce and Alan paid for lunch again in August, when we had our first $2-million month, and again in October, when we had our first $3-million month. Although we started the year with WordPerfect in only 15 percent of the computer retail stores, we ended it with our product carried in practically every store. Everywhere we went, dealers wanted to sell WordPerfect.

About one-third of our sales were in the Washington, D.C. area. While I'm inclined to criticize the decision-making abilities of our government, they—to their credit—discovered WordPerfect when it was still practically unknown. Forced by federal purchasing guidelines to evaluate most products, they gave us the highest rating in almost all of their evaluations. Individuals would buy more WordStar in 1985, and large businesses would buy more Multimate, but government offices and agencies would buy more WordPerfect.

Keeping up with our growth was a big problem. Our informal management style worked well when eighty people were focused on getting 4.0 out the door, but it was breaking down under the weight of all the new people we had to hire. Crisis growth worked fine for office space and computers, and management-by-luncheon helped improve communications among departments, but our biggest problems were their operations. Each department had the freedom to design its own organization and set its own policies. Everyone solved their problems by trial-and-error, and we had all kinds of inefficiencies creeping into the company. The orders department, for example, seemed to keep a copier running full-time. When I asked why, they said they were making extra invoice copies to be filed by number, by customer, and by product. When asked why, they said they weren't sure, except that it had always been done that way. To make a point, I threw one full set in the trash and told them to call me if they ever missed the extra copies.

As we hired new people, we generally tried to keep

the number of management levels to a minimum to maintain a "flat" organization, but the number of managers we used varied considerably from department to department. Our developers, for example, had a very flat organization: All of them answered directly to Alan Ashton. At the other extreme, the customer support department had seventeen employees, of whom more than half were managers or assistant managers.

Our hiring methods were also inconsistent. We had no interviewing standards, no policies for hiring or not hiring friends or relatives, and we rarely checked references. Almost everyone who hired somebody made promises about raises and future opportunities without writing anything down, and we all tended to describe job opportunities as more glamorous than they were. These unkept promises made for a lot of unhappy people.

To make matters worse, new employees were given almost no training, very little supervision, and in general, did not understand how their jobs fit into the bigger company picture. We told people that our basic management philosophy was to "teach people correct principles and let them govern themselves," but we did very little teaching. We were much better at turning people loose than we were at helping them learn what it was we needed them to do.

I spent a lot of time trying to figure out how to fix these problems. I knew we needed better training and more supervision, but I wasn't exactly sure how to achieve these results. Deciding who should do the supervising particularly bothered me. I didn't see how I could make everyone happy, if I asked some to supervise and didn't ask others.

Whenever I got stuck, I called my dad in California. He had been a vice president of marketing for a division of Harris Corporation and had much more experience than I did running a large organization. I explained our problems, and he told me a story he had heard years before at a management seminar. I would think about this story many times over the next few years.

The tale concerned a good king, his knights, and his prime minister. The knights of the kingdom were brave and loyal. They loved to jump on white chargers and rush off to slay dragons or save damsels. The knights performed their feats with very little planning and rarely did their postfeat paperwork, but they made up for these shortcomings with their fearlessness, their strength, and their energy. The king was also lucky to have a very good prime minister. The minister saw that taxes were collected, that the majority of the revenues were wisely spent to improve the kingdom, and that the excess monies were well managed.

One day the prime minister died, and the king asked his bravest and most fearless knight to be the new minister. Unfortunately, the knight chosen for the job liked jumping on his white charger more than he liked caring for the affairs of the kingdom. He continued to gallop off to slay dragons whenever he had the opportunity and neglected tax collections, investments, improvements, and repairs. After only a short time, the king ran out of money, the peasants ran out of patience, and the kingdom collapsed.

My dad compared the brave knights to the very best marketing and development employees. These people loved to jump on airplanes or into impossible situations to save the day by closing big sales or inventing something new. Their first response was to act, and results were their primary concern. They used a Ready, Fire, Aim approach and in many cases were successful.

Unfortunately, this approach failed if a problem required careful planning or attention to small details. Brave knights generally did poorly when assigned to management positions. They were always too busy and too involved in the current crisis to spend much time supervising others or planning for the future. They lacked the patience to stick around long enough to train and support their people.

Good prime ministers made better managers than did knights. Their first course of action was to think, and their primary concern was to come up with a good plan before they wasted a lot of energy. They stayed late to finish the paperwork and always knew how much money they were spending.

This story helped me begin to understand the magnitude of the problem we were facing. A company needs its superstars, but it also needs good managers, who make careful decisions, who pay close attention to details, and who care enough about the people they supervise to dedicate some time to them. If we were to be successful over the long term, our superstars would either have to take the time and trouble required to become good supervisors or let others take over.

In our case, we were a company filled with superstars. We had all worked on impossible problems and had all made significant contributions to the company's success. We had enjoyed the freedom to run our own areas of the company as we wanted, and few of us felt we needed any more supervision. If there was to be a new structure to the organization, we all wanted to be at the top. My dad suggested we consider limiting the size of the company and try to avoid the problem altogether. In all his years of experience, he had yet to see a knight turn into a good prime minister.

I was discouraged enough to ask Alan if perhaps we should be more cautious and put a cap on the number of our employees. Neither of us had dreamed the company would grow so quickly. Though our sales were increasing, our expenses were increasing as well. The responsibility of meeting these expenses was an enormous weight on our shoulders. As a result, I think we were ready to slow things down a little.

On the night after our conversation, I had a dream. I was in the reception area of our offices standing knee-deep in money. There were three or four other people in the room with me, and together we were trying to pick up the money and stuff it into bags as quickly as possible. I remember wishing we had more people to help us. The money was ours to take if only we could pick it up.

This dream was not too far removed from what the software business was actually like for us. It reminded me that the opportunity was there for the taking, if we didn't lose our nerve and back off. I told Alan about my dream the next morning and told him that I no longer wanted to put a limit on our growth. Opportunity was not just knocking, it was breaking down our door. All we had to do was get out of the way.

From that time on, I felt like WordPerfect had a life of its own and that I was merely a spectator to an amazing phenomenon. I realized that I had no way of predicting or controlling how big the company would get in the next few years, but while I could not control its size, I was going to try my best to control its shape and structure. I saw myself as an architect, with the responsibility to keep the organization flat and efficient, with the fewest number of management layers possible.

I wasn't sure if Bruce and Alan wanted me to take on this responsibility, but I did it anyway. As a college student, I had worked two summers for government contractors and observed real bureaucracies firsthand. Remembering my experiences, I was determined that SSI would not fall into the same unproductive traps that my early employers had. These corporations were full of organizational charts, formal lines of communication and authority, and much wasted time and effort. My habit of getting to work on time and getting a fast start was discouraged by most other employees. The work was done in bits and pieces, when it did not interfere with taking breaks, eating lunch, playing bridge, talking sports, participating in betting pools, bringing each other up-to-date on our personal lives, celebrating birthdays, or watching and commenting on the girls in the office. As a young idealist, I had hated working at a slow pace in order to fit in with the rest of the guys.

Working for Don had a lot to do with the way I felt about supervisors and helped to shape my beliefs as to how supervision should be handled in an organization. During my first year at SSI, my financial duties took up only a small amount of my time. I spent the majority of it as Don's assistant. When he was out of the office, I served as a messenger between him and our clients. When he was in the office, I did whatever he told me to do for the day. When I wrote a letter, I signed his name at the bottom. Any training I got came in the form of lessons given when I messed up or did too much on my own. I felt like a little kid who couldn't go out to play because his mom wanted him at her side in case she had an errand for him to run. Once Don left, I enjoyed working without someone looking over my shoulder. I came to the conclusion that working without a supervisor was better than working for an overattentive one.

Taking on the role of company architect didn't help my image much. I was already the designated bad guy on the board. Bruce spent much of his time in Europe, and when he was in the office, he was either working on international issues or helping with development problems. Alan was always nice and agreeable and preferred to avoid contention. He was much better at smoothing ruffled feathers and settling disputes than he was at handing out bad news. That left me to say no, if no had to be said.

Because I watched over the finances and jealously guarded the distribution of our money, anyone wanting to try a new program or hire a new employee had to come to me. I played the role of the sheriff in a Wild West town, where most of the town's citizens were unsure they wanted a sheriff. Bringing some sort of financial law and order to the company while attempting to maintain a flat organization meant disappointing a lot of people.

A flat structure by its nature is bound to discourage some, because it limits management opportunities. If you have an organization that requires two hundred people to do its work, and if the supervisors in the company each have no more than five people reporting to them, then you will need approximately fifty supervisors. This tall type of structure will likely have a president, two to four vice presidents, five to ten directors, and forty managers. Counting the two hundred employees who do the actual work, you will have five layers in the company.

If you were to change the number of people one person supervised from five to twenty, you would create a much flatter structure. In theory, you would need only a president and ten managers. This would reduce the number of layers in the company to three and the number of managers to eleven. Not only would this flatter organization be likely to function more efficiently, but the company would also save the salaries of thirty-nine managers.

In reality, eleven managers for two hundred people is not likely to be enough. Not all departments and functions break down to exactly twenty people each, and not every manager is likely to have the experience and skill to help and support twenty people. Still, a company this size should be able to function very well with no more than twenty to twenty-five managers and no more than four layers.

Within a flat structure, the management opportunities are probably less than half those found in a tall structure, so the odds of moving up the management ladder are much lower. If our sample company were to grow to the point where one thousand employees were required, a tall organization would need to add two hundred managers, while the flat one would need only forty-three. There is room for everyone to move up in the

tall organization, but in the flat organization there is
room for only one in five.

For those who joined SSI to move up a career ladder,
this flat structure was a source of tremendous frustration,
and their frustration was generally directed at me. If employees needed help to get all their work done, they usually wanted to hire assistants. Instead of letting them
hire subordinates, which would create another layer in
the company, I asked them to give up part of their responsibilities. If we needed new employees to take those
responsibilities, the new people would be hired as peers
rather than as subordinates.

For example, Doug Lloyd, the salesman we hired
away from IBM, at one time had responsibility for all
large accounts, including large corporations, federal
agencies, and schools. As we grew, he had more work
than he could handle, and we turned his government
and school accounts over to two other people. Later,
when he needed help with corporate accounts, we gave
two-thirds of his accounts to two others. In both cases,
the people who were given a part of Doug's responsibilities became his peers, reporting to the same supervisor
he did.

For most people, and especially for the company superstars, losing responsibility was very discouraging.
Not only were they not moving up in the organization,
but they viewed their losses as demotions. Instead of having more and more assistants, they saw themselves as
having more and more rivals. How could they explain
to their spouses or parents that because they were doing
a great job, they had to give up responsibilities?

I came to believe that I would have to live with my
share of enemies inside the company if we were going to
keep a flat organization. As more supervision became
necessary, I made additional enemies. Some people who
had reported directly to the board felt slighted when
asked to report to a supervisor a step below the board.
Although I tried to ease the pain with a good explana-

tion or by handing out new and better titles, there were always a few people who couldn't understand why the company's growth didn't give them a more important or more prestigious role.

Many believed that my reason for promoting a flat structure was so I could exercise greater personal control. While I didn't agree that my preference was to promote my own self-interest, I agreed that a flat organization concentrates more authority in the hands of fewer people. It also promotes better communication within an organization, because there are not as many layers to filter the information.

In spite of our problems and my efforts to solve them, 1985 was proving to be another great year for SSI. Sales of WordPerfect for DOS were going through the roof, overshadowing the fact that our other products could hardly make it out the door. Ironically, we were as determined as ever to develop more products—even if many of them were unsuccessful.

WordPerfect jr and MathPlan jr sold as poorly as IBM's PC jr, which was a miserable failure. Not only did we fail with WordPerfect jr in English, but we went ahead and failed in Danish and Norwegian as well. Personal WordPerfect, designed to compete with PFS:Write and to fill a gap between the full version of WordPerfect and our jr version, sold very few copies. Sales of Math-Plan for DOS and MathPlan for AOS went nowhere. SSI*Legal, Lew Bastian's legal-time-and-billing package; SSI*FORTH, our first and last programming language; and SSI*Data, our poorly received database all had disappointing sales. P-Edit was still around and selling poorly. Luckily, we came to our senses before releasing TranSSIt, deciding not to ship the low-priced communications package because the support costs were likely to be too high for us to show a profit.

The one new product that did sell well was our Apple II version of WordPerfect. Although we might have made a lot more money with a Macintosh version, we started out so far behind on the Mac that we decided to finish our Apple II version first. We were too small a company to get the kind of attention and help from Apple that Microsoft was getting. Bill Gates had already tilted the Macintosh software playing field so much in his favor that we were discouraged about our prospects in the new market. Unfortunately, we would not release WordPerfect for the Macintosh until 1988, giving Microsoft Word for the Mac a four-year head start.

Looking back, it's easy to see we were trying to develop and sell too many products too quickly, but we were as determined as ever to be more than a one-product company. Even though our 1985 sales would more than double our 1984 sales, we felt a considerable amount of embarrassment because we could not produce another best- or even good-selling product.

We could have saved ourselves a lot of headaches by concentrating on fewer products. For every product we released, we had to manufacture a standard retail version, an update version for customers who had purchased the previous release, a demonstration version for dealers, a special version to give away, a low-priced version for schools, and versions manufactured especially for large corporate and government customers. Not only did we have to prepare and keep track of these complete packages, but we had to make the templates and manuals available separately. In addition to our American English products, we had to make similar but different English packages for our Canadian, British, and Australian customers. We also made two sets for our French-speaking customers in France and Canada, and additional sets for all the other international languages we supported. We did not make our mistakes one a time; we made them twenty at a time.

Developing the software and the software packages was, of course, only part of the work. We had to figure out how to price the products and how to roll them out. We had to come up with the brochures, advertisements, and promotions. Then we had to spend hours and months trying to figure out what we were doing wrong when the products didn't sell. It was rarely appropriate to blame the developers if a product did poorly. We always had to keep searching for a marketing solution to our failures.

Fortunately, we had the foresight to save enough of our time and resources to get WordPerfect 4.1 ready for release in the fall of 1985. This version was not thrown together at the last minute, the way 4.0 was. We were now involved in what the press called a features race— a race we knew we could win. The new version had at least one-hundred new features, including an automatic table of contents, automatic indexing, footnotes that could spill over to the next page, paragraph numbering, an improved speller, and a thesaurus. All the new features were written by our own programmers, unlike our competitors, who looked to other companies for things like thesauruses and spellers. Not only did we save money by doing all the work ourselves, but all the features we built functioned similarly and worked well together.

Our key strengths had always been our programmers and our ability to keep them from leaving the company. When some of our competitors finished a product, their programmers seemed to scatter like pins after a strike in a bowling alley. It usually took them months to line up a new programming team to work on an update version of an existing product. We kept our teams intact, however, so we lost no time between releases.

The changeover from 4.0 to 4.1 was a big manufacturing challenge, because this was the first time we were dealing with large numbers. Sales of $2 million meant that about one hundred thousand copies of WordPerfect were shipped each month. That was a lot of paper, binders, and disks for a company doing things by trial-and-error.

Our biggest concern was making sure we did not end up with extra copies of version 4.0. During the mid-1980s, as soon as a new version came out, the old version became obsolete. If we ended up with fifty thousand 4.0 copies too many, for example, we would lose $1 million. If we ended up with fifty thousand too few, we would be out of product and out of sales for two weeks. Hitting the number right on was difficult, because the 4.1 release date was a moving target.

As the 4.1 release date neared we became very nervous. With 3.0 and 4.0, we had experienced a sales slowdown just prior to release, as word of the release leaked out from our beta test sites. We factored this slowdown into our estimates, and for the first and only time, word of the new release did not leak out. Our sales were increasing at a time when they should have been decreasing, and we were in danger of running out of WordPerfect for DOS for about a month.

Our security was so good that I was forced to ask someone inside our company to call Spencer Katt, the writer of the rumors column at *PC Week*, to spread the news of our upcoming release through the industry grapevine. Once news of 4.1 appeared in *PC Week*, sales of 4.0 dropped back below $2 million a month, and we were out of product for less than two weeks. Our entire marketing department was so angry about the security leak that I waited a few months before I told them that I was the culprit.

Once 4.1 was released, our October sales jumped to more than $3 million. We could have sold more that month, but our sales estimates were low and our printing company didn't have the capacity to meet an increase in our orders. For the first time, we had to ration our product to distributors. WordPerfect 4.1 would be in short supply until the first of the year, when we hired more printers.

COMDEX that year was a lot of fun. Mark and Sherry, our professional actors from Chicago, were back doing another song-and-dance presentation. They added slides to their show, featuring screen shots of many of 4.1's new features. There was so much interest in our new version that we no longer had to drag people into our booth: People sought us out and told us how much they liked our product.

We ended the year with sales of $23 million, two-and-a-half times those of 1984. That made us the number-two word processor, because Ashton-Tate had acquired Multimate, and its sales had leveled off at $20 million. Only WordStar was ahead of us, but we were right on their tail. Their quarterly sales were down to only $10 million, and ours were up to $9 million. At Softsel, one of the two largest distributors, we were already outselling WordStar.

Our pretax profits were up to 25 percent, so we were starting to make enough money to play the software game like professionals. With *InfoWorld* giving us another perfect score for WordPerfect 4.1, we knew 1986 would be another great year for SSI. Although we could feel the growing pains which accompanied our increase from eighty-four people to almost two hundred, we looked like a company that knew what it was doing and where it was going.

# 7

# AWKWARD
# ADOLESCENCE

---

By now we had our software business down to a simple routine. Every year, we released a new version of Word-Perfect, and every year we doubled our sales. It was almost as easy as printing money on our own printing press. Except for two small clouds on the horizon, our future looked bright.

Almost everything having to do with 4.1 went smoothly. At first we billed it as a minor release, because 4.0 was doing so well. We were afraid that if we made a big deal, we might scare some companies into thinking that 4.1 was very different from 4.0. Often, when a significantly different version of a product was released, a company would conduct formal evaluations of the product to determine whether they would use the upgrade or switch to another product, and we hoped they would decide an evaluation was unnecessary. We didn't want to disrupt their purchasing patterns now that they were already buying from us.

Our customers quickly saw through our "minor release" strategy, but they didn't slow their purchases. They were crazy about it. The first quarter that 4.1 was available—the fourth quarter of 1985—our sales jumped more than 50 percent over our best previous quarter. After the *InfoWorld* review, sales went up to $10 million for the first quarter of 1986. We were now in a dead heat with WordStar and had enough momentum to pass them. Our only problem was filling all the orders. The local printing companies couldn't print the manuals quickly enough to keep up with the demand, which sometimes created a six-week backlog for update copies. As a result of the 4.1 rush, our PC market share was now somewhere between 20 percent and 25 percent.

Once WordStar was almost out of our way, we were ready to set our sights on other competitors. For the short-term, Wang was still an important player in the word-processing industry. Personal computers could not yet match all of the capabilities available on the larger Wang machines, especially in the areas of networking and security, and many of Wang's customers felt they could not afford to abandon their sizable investments in Wang equipment. Law firms were especially loyal to the old machines, because many lawyers were not ready to have computers on their desks. They liked the old method of dictating their documents to their secretaries and having final versions produced by the firm's word-processing center.

Wang was trying desperately to keep its business growing. It was a multibillion-dollar company, accustomed to profits greater than those brought in by the entire PC word-processing software industry. Little, multimillion-dollar companies like Micropro and SSI were devouring its business, but Wang was not prepared to cut its size quickly enough to compete in the personal computer market. It was a dinosaur, unwilling to adapt to the new environment, and all that was left for it to do was to survive until its money ran out.

Another big competitor in the short-term was IBM's Displaywrite. Most of the dedicated word-processing companies like CPT, Dictaphone, Lanier, NBI, and Wang had not been able to make a transition to the PC word-processing world. Many had decided to close up shop rather than compete in the new, low-priced market. Some, like Wang, had chosen to ignore the PC and continue on as if nothing had changed. A few companies, notably NBI and IBM, had tried to write software for the PC, but had not been able to sell many copies. IBM was the only company from the dedicated word-processing world that also had a significant market share in the PC word-processing world. They didn't publish their software sales figures, but we were fairly sure IBM's market share was close to ours. Displaywrite was usually found to be an inferior product by the press and by IBM's customers; nonetheless, IBM continued to sell a lot of software. There was still some magic left in the IBM name.

In the long-term, Microsoft was the only significant threat to our money-making machine. They were the only competitor we had that had the resources, talent, endurance, and understanding to write a good PC product. Micropro had the resources and the endurance, but was famous for losing its talented programmers. Ashton-Tate also had the resources, but similarly could not keep good programmers. Lotus had most of the qualifications to write a good product, but didn't understand the market. This spreadsheet maker wrote a word processor aimed at the technical user that instead missed everyone. IBM had more than enough resources and endurance, but couldn't write good software. IBM shuffled its programmers in and out of large programming teams; they based evaluations of team performance on the quantity of lines of code written rather than the quality of the code. At one point, they broke up the entire Displaywrite development team by moving the project from Texas to New York. If Beethoven could have written a good symphony by putting one hundred composers in a room and requiring each to write ten musical phrases that he would later piece together, then perhaps IBM could have written good software. I don't think IBM understood that creating beautiful software, like creating beautiful music, was an art form and not a manufacturing challenge.

Although Microsoft had a better appreciation of how to write good software, they had too many irons in the fire in 1986 to concentrate on our market very much. They were much larger than we were, but we always had at least three times as many programmers devoted to word processing. Perhaps what held them back more than their lack of resources was their arrogance—believing they were smarter than everyone else. As a group of intellectuals holding degrees from the most prestigious institutions, they had trouble believing BYU graduate students could beat them. On one occasion, one of their programmers watched a demonstration given by Bruce at our COMDEX booth. He interrupted Bruce, telling him that some of the things he was demonstrating were impossible. It took real arrogance for that programmer to dispute something he could see with his own eyes, and it was this kind of arrogance that showed in Microsoft's product.

For 1986, we set our sights on IBM and Wang and directed practically all of our marketing efforts toward large accounts, believing that if we could capture them, then schools and small businesses would follow their lead. All of our advertising was aimed directly at large corporations. Our reps still visited dealers, but didn't spend as much time doing so. We provided big companies with free demonstration copies, extra telephone support, and special pricing. We let them know that we either offered products or intended to offer products for IBM's entire line of computers.

IBM helped us win over many of its customers. Since 1983, we had offered WordPerfect directly to IBM employees for $125 a copy, and more IBM employees probably used WordPerfect than used Displaywrite at home. In 1984, we let IBM offices buy WordPerfect at the same low price. Until 1989, when IBM forbade its offices to use it without written permission, WordPerfect was probably on as many machines in IBM offices as was Display-write. Around 1983, IBM started buying our software as a distributor, reselling WordPerfect to its own custom-ers. Even though IBM preferred to sell its product, many of the company's employees and offices recommended ours.

While these recommendations helped, the biggest fa-vor IBM did for us was to offer few improvements on their product over the years. IBM's customers wanted to remain loyal and were willing to put up with poor per-formance and an awkward interface, but we were adding too many new features for those customers to stay with Displaywrite. Each new release of WordPerfect put more pressure on a company's decision-makers to dump Dis-playwrite. IBM couldn't improve its product quickly enough to prevent its customers from jumping ship.

If the computing world had stayed as it was in 1986, we would have had little trouble from our competition. There were, however, two big changes coming that would eventually give Microsoft a chance to catch us. The first was the laser printer and the second was the graphical user interface, or GUI (pronounced "gooey"). Both were still only small threats to our business, but support for them would require an enormous amount of work. It was a little discouraging to realize that just as we were beginning to win the word-processing game, the rules were changing.

Adapting to these new rules left our programmers no time to enjoy the success of 4.1. Laser printers were start-ing to sell, and our three-year-old printing technology was not capable of supporting the new printers well. We could produce a document that looked like it was type-written, but we couldn't produce a document that looked like it came from a printing company. We were limited to only eight fonts in a document and only one font on a line. Our proportional spacing support was not perfect, and our program had no provision for kerning (the process of fitting proportionally spaced letters closer together) or leading (adjusting the space between lines). The program also had no support for graphics (pictures, figures, or drawings). To support these features, we had to redesign and rewrite the entire printing portion of the program and much of the screen portion. It was like 3.0 all over again, only this time the job was huge.

Every function code in the document needed to be changed. All measurements, including the ones for margins and tabs, needed to be in inches or centimeters, instead of lines and spaces. Fonts needed names and point sizes, like Helvetica 14 point. WordPerfect needed to learn how to download fonts to printers and how to support font cartridges. It needed to know the width and height of every character in every font.

By February we knew we would never finish the project to meet a fall COMDEX deadline. We were afraid of the consequences if we broke our routine of having a new version ready for the show, so we decided to split our developers into two groups. The smaller of the two groups worked on 4.1L, a version to be released in fall 1986, which would use the old printing technology. The other group worked on WordPerfect 5.0, which would include the new printing capabilities. We hoped that 5.0 would be ready for release in fall of 1987.

The "L" in the 4.1L stood for *legal,* because it was aimed at the legal industry. We hoped that 4.1L would get us into more law offices and that new features for line numbering, improved paragraph numbering, and an automatic table of authorities would be the last nails in Wang's coffin. For customers outside the legal market, the release of 4.1L would truly be a minor event.

Neither of the new versions included support for a graphical user interface, because we didn't have the resources to improve both the printing and add GUI. Of

the two technologies, our customers were more interested in support for the laser printer, and that provided
more than enough work to keep our developers busy
through 1987. We could only hope that the impending
GUI revolution would take some time to catch on.

There was no clear GUI-environment winner in
1986. IBM with TopView, Microsoft with Windows, and
Digital Research (the CP/M guys were still around) with
Gem were all trying to become the GUI of choice on the
IBM PC platform. We were pulling for anyone but Microsoft to win. They were the company most likely to
give us trouble in the future, and we didn't want them
in control of the GUI environment.

Whenever a customer or a reporter asked me if we
intended to support Windows, I liked to compare Microsoft to the fox in the story of the Gingerbread Man. In
the fairy tale, the Gingerbread Man jumps from the oven
and runs away from the old couple that baked him. The
old farmers try to catch him, but he yells the famous line,
"Run, run as fast as you can, but you can't catch me, I'm
the Gingerbread Man." As he runs away, he passes many
animals who try to eat him, but he runs away from each
animal, repeating the line "Run, run as fast as you can
. . ." Unfortunately, he comes up short when he reaches
a river. At the river, he meets a fox, who offers to take
him across the river so he can escape his pursuers. Although he's wary of the fox, the Gingerbread Man jumps
on his back and accepts the ride, believing the fox's
promise not to eat him. Halfway across the river, the fox
lets his back sink into the water and, claiming weakness,
asks the Gingerbread Man to jump onto his shoulders.
The fox sinks lower in the water, forcing the Gingerbread Man to move to the top of the fox's head and,
eventually, to the tip of his nose. Just before the Gingerbread Man reaches the safety of the opposite shore, the
fox opens his mouth and gobbles him up.

WordPerfect was like the Gingerbread Man, running
to stay ahead of the competition by adding more and

more features each year. When we came to the GUI river, Microsoft asked us to trust them and let them take us safely to the other side. They approached us, as well as a number of other popular software companies, under the guise of collaboration. They offered us help if, in return, we would develop a version of WordPerfect for Windows. While we knew Microsoft wanted Windows to succeed—a feat requiring the development of Windows-based applications—we realized there was little chance that they wanted us to beat them in the word-processing market. In spite of their assurances that Windows, rather than word processing, was their top priority, I didn't think I could trust them. I had trouble understanding how they could keep a straight face while giving us their sales pitch. They were an aggressive company, and their appetite for success knew no bounds. They were a sly, rich, hungry, and intelligent fox. I was not going to encourage SSI to accept their offer if there was any hope that another company might give us a ride across the river.

By the spring of 1986, we were starting to do fairly well in western Europe. We had versions of WordPerfect for every western European country expect Italy and Portugal, and those translations were in the works. Our royalties from our European distributors amounted to about $5 million a year, and at least $3 million of that was profit. Although we were not well-known in England, Germany, and France, we were enjoying significant market shares in most of the other European countries. In some of the Scandinavian countries, we had market shares greater than 50 percent.

Now that we were a $40-million company, there were times when I felt a little overwhelmed. Believing I had to know more if I was going to run a large corporation effectively, I applied and was accepted at BYU's executive M.B.A. program. I decided not to go, however, once I realized SSI was likely to be a $100-million company before I was even halfway through the program. For better or worse, I would have to rely on what I could learn from books and from the job.

I continued to go to my dad for help, and Dan Lunt and I flew to California to listen to what he had to say. He had done a lot of formal planning at Harris and offered to help us understand the process he had used. He showed us a very complicated flowchart that described his planning process. In the first step, a company defined its purpose, goals, and objectives. The next step required the company to predict how well it would do in meeting its goals and objectives if no changes were made to future plans. If the company's predictions fell short of the goals and objectives—which was usually the case—then the third step was to determine how to improve performance. Depending on the time frame, the company might increase or improve its development or marketing efforts, or it might consider acquiring other products or other companies. My dad emphasized that each of the steps required good communication from the top to the bottom of the organization. This communication ensured that everyone in the company understood and agreed to the purpose, goals, and objectives, that the forecasts were accurate, and that everyone would try to make the new marketing, development, or acquisition plan work.

The approach was entirely new to me. For one thing, we started each year without any specific sales goals. Bruce and Alan never asked for a number, and I enjoyed not having to be responsible for one. I was also afraid that focusing on an arbitrary sales goal would hurt rather than help. I thought if we focused instead on working hard and doing a good job we could succeed. Success is measured by expectations, and I wanted us to feel successful if we did our best and worked well together. I did not want us to get discouraged if our numbers ended up 2 percent short of some prediction we made.

We also had no thoughts of acquiring other products

or other companies. I liked to keep things simple; it was the only way I could deal with the complexities of running the business. We had enough trouble writing, selling, and supporting our own products without having to integrate another company or another product line. I didn't want to ask for problems we didn't know how to solve.

Although much of the process my dad explained didn't apply to us, it was obvious we needed a written definition of our purpose and objectives. It was no surprise that our employees had trouble understanding how the company worked and what they were expected to do: We never told them. We could live without the sales goals and the acquisitions, but we definitely needed to publish and teach what it was we were trying to accomplish.

As we set out to define these things, it became obvious that we needed to change our name. Satellite Software International didn't fit and certainly didn't tell the world what we were doing. SSI Software was only a small improvement. WordPerfect, Inc., was the obvious choice, especially if we ever intended to focus on word processing, but for years Dan had rejected the name because of the way it sounded on the telephone. If someone wasn't careful about their pronunciation, WordPerfect sounded like "we're perfect." We considered names like Artistry Software, Futuresoft, ProSoft, and even Image Resource Company. We finally gave up, however, deciding instead to be careful about our pronunciation. In 1986 we officially became WordPerfect Corporation. We used the word *corporation,* because it was about the same length as WordPerfect, and the two words looked good together, with one on top of the other.

By now our employees were scattered all over the city of Orem. The customer support department was located a mile to the southeast of our main offices, grabbing practically every square foot of Lincoln Square office park. The number of support calls had jumped to eight thousand a week with the release of 4.1 and continued to rise as sales increased. The accounting and publications departments—along with SoftCopy, our manufacturing company—were about one mile to the northeast and were expanding as well. The Macintosh, Amiga, Atari, and VAX groups were all at the very south end of Orem, and the DG group would move across and just down the street from our main offices. By the end of the year, we had more than three hundred people in the company at eight different sites.

There were some advantages to being spread out. The distances forced the department managers to take on more responsibilities and solve more of their problems themselves. We also saved a lot of money. If we had tried to build a facility big enough to house the entire company, we would have had to borrow money or find investors, both of which were against our nature.

We were, however, at a point where we could afford to begin building a complex that would bring the company together again. The most promising site was in northeast Orem. The city had purchased a 110-acre orchard in a residential section and had used federal matching funds to put in the improvements for a business park. In spite of the objections of the surrounding residents, the city officials intended to build and lease office buildings in the park and use the profits from the venture to increase the city's tax base. We liked the location, but when they offered us space in 1985, we did not like the terms. Instead of offering incentives to move in as some neighboring cities did, Orem was requiring a very long lease at what we thought was a high price. No other companies were interested either. Novell, which had been the most sought-after company for the park, had moved to Provo instead. The orchard had a beautiful infrastructure with streets, sidewalks, streetlights, electricity, water, and a sewer system, but it had no tenants. Besides the fruit, the primary benefit of the park was to give local teenagers a secluded place to park late at night.

Late in the summer of 1986, I called the city to see if they were desperate enough to abandon the lease requirements and sell us a few acres outright. I offered to pay $25,000 per acre if we could own the land. After some negotiating, they agreed to let us buy twenty-two acres for about $22,000 per acre, if we would agree to certain other conditions. We eventually purchased about 95 percent of the park and built a number of buildings on the site, though we would add buildings only as we had the money.

In August of 1986, 4.1L was close to completion, but much to our chagrin, one of the trade publications leaked the story of the release before we were ready to ship. It was probably only fair, after the way we had used the press to slow down the sales of 4.0, but we were still upset. We weren't prepared for sales to go down in anticipation of a new release. We decided to change the version number to 4.2, if for no other reason than to make the publication look bad.

We also added a few more features. Alan Ashton, Doug Lloyd, Layne Cannon (a programmer and another former student of Alan's), and I had taken 4.1L on the road to show to four or five of our largest accounts. After looking it over, these customers all wanted more. They were willing to wait another year for 5.0, if we were willing to add a few more features to 4.1L. Most of the changes were fairly easy to make, like increasing the number of columns supported and adding two new types of tabs. We added them in about thirty days and were still ready to release by COMDEX.

The changes made our manual a lot more interesting. Originally, a few update pages would have handled all of the 4.1L changes, but with the 4.2 additions, we needed a new manual. Unfortunately, we didn't have enough time to produce one. At first, we sent out the old 4.1 manual with update pages which the customer had to insert himself. It was difficult for customer support to deal with two manuals—the one with update pages and

the new one—but we felt we had to ship before COM-
DEX to maintain good sales.

We hoped that no one would care too much about
our laser printing deficiencies, but Microsoft was too sly
to let that happen. Laser printers were becoming more
popular every day, and Microsoft supported them better
than we did. They did a good job making sure our customers found out about our weakness; yet, despite their
propaganda, our sales didn't decline. Third quarter
shipments had jumped to almost $14 million, and with
the release of 4.2, they would jump again to almost $18
million.

The dark clouds on the horizon—laser printing and
GUI—looked less ominous once 4.2 was released. Microsoft was having trouble releasing a good version of Windows, and our customers weren't impatient for fancy
fonts in their documents. It looked as if we would have
time to catch up.

As in years past, we were not content to sell only a
DOS version of WordPerfect, and we now had many
other versions. Microsoft was betting that the larger
computers would go away. They had Word versions for
the PC and the Mac, and they were working on a Windows version, but they had not publicly indicated that
they were putting their word processor on more machines. Although we were inclined to agree that larger
machines were not too important in the long-term, we
did think that supporting them in the short-term would
help companies choose WordPerfect as their standard.
We wanted to be the world's word-processing standard,
and we hoped to support all of the significant computing platforms. In 1986 we had software released or in the
works for Digital Equipment's VAX, IBM's mainframes,
Data General's minicomputers, and many UNIX machines. In addition to these big machines, we had software released for the Apple II and software in the works
for Apple IIGS, Macintosh, Amiga, and Atari. We were
also still supporting many of the old DOS machines that

were not IBM PC compatible, as well as many different types of PC networks.

We weren't very careful about how we made a decision to support a new platform. At times, we seemed completely out of our minds. For example, we started the Amiga project because a few of our Apple II and Macintosh programmers were sneaking source code out of the office, so they could translate it at home for the Amiga. Their plan was to surprise us with a finished product for us to sell. When Alan, Bruce, and I discovered that our programmers felt strongly enough about the Amiga to port WordPerfect on their own time, we assumed that enough other people wanted to use the machine as well. We should have done at least a little research or taken a little more time with the decision. By continuing the Amiga project, we were taking on work which had little chance of showing a profit.

The DG division benefited from our efforts to have WordPerfect running on every platform that made sense. The DG group had been neglected for years, and was now allowed to hire enough programmers to bring WordPerfect up-to-date on that platform. They were also given enough resources to think about writing an office automation package.

Office automation (OA) was the hot product in the early 1980s, when large computers ruled the world. The goal had been a paperless office, one in which all employees had computer terminals on their desks and in which documents were written, memos were sent, and meetings were scheduled electronically using one software package. Wang had Wang Office, Data General had CEO (Comprehensive Electronic Office), DEC had All-in-One, IBM had PROFS, and the list went on. The OA market did fairly well until the PC came along. Then the automated office was temporarily forgotten, as most customers decided they cared more about 1-2-3 than they did about electronic messages.

Our DG programmers were interested in office

automation because one of their word-processing clients, the United States Department of Justice, was interested in it. Thinking they had to provide electronic mail and electronic scheduling to keep the DOJ's word-processing business, the DG crew began work on an OA system they called Library.

The DOS group was interested in the work the DG group was doing. They had also released a product called Library, which was a collection of DOS programs that we couldn't figure out how to sell separately. The collection, which cost $129, included a shell, which let the user list and start DOS programs by means of a menu, an editor (P-Edit), a calculator, a file manager (for finding files), a simple database, a calendar, and a game called Beast. We didn't expect to make a lot of money; rather, that our customers could get good use out of the programs. The DOS Library programmers hoped to turn their program into an office automation package for PC networks by adding electronic mail and enhancing the calendar to be able to schedule meetings.

For a relatively small company, we were certainly involved in a lot of different things. We intended to offer a word processor, a spreadsheet, a database, and an office automation package for all the successful computers, while commanding a significant market share. We also asked Dave Moon, who had worked on MathPlan and Library, to look into desktop publishing. We were probably as aggressive as Microsoft in our development plans, but we didn't feel as greedy, since we limited ourselves to applications. We seemed determined to try every software applications category until we found another winner.

Unfortunately, we never seemed to find a way to sell these other products in large volume. With MathPlan, for example, we tried increasing its advertising and dropping its price to $195, but sales didn't go up. We also tried a $99 MathPlan promotion for WordPerfect users, but the promotion fizzled after one month. These and other failures encouraged a lot of finger pointing, with marketing claiming that we needed more features and developers saying that we needed better advertising. I thought the problem was that we never committed enough programming resources to these other products to make them successful. Alan and Bruce thought the products were good enough to sell well if we were more aggressive with our marketing. I had trouble believing we should spend more money on products that had already been given a reasonable chance of succeeding.

Fall COMDEX was again better than ever, and by now, André was turning into a real showman. He had constructed a large game wheel for the show, one which required the approval of the Nevada Gaming Commission. During each show, our actors invited four or five members of the audience to come up on stage and spin the wheel to win a prize. Since our products were the prizes, it gave us a chance to draw some attention to our other programs. André's idea worked. Our COMDEX booth was packed with people pushing and shoving to get a seat.

Near the end of the year, I received my copy of *InfoWorld* containing their review of WordPerfect 4.2. I now had a ritual for reading the review: I would take the magazine home and wait until everyone else in the house was asleep. Then, in a comfortable chair, I would very slowly read and enjoy every word of the review. There was not much enjoyment this year, however. Although the review was very positive, we did not receive a perfect score. *InfoWorld* had toughened their standards and marked us down because of our printing deficiencies.

We finished the year with $52 million in sales and pretax profits of almost $15 million. This made us the fifth largest PC computer software company, behind Microsoft, Lotus, Novell, and Ashton-Tate, but more importantly, it made us the king of the word-processing hill. The ground that had been held by IBM from 1964 to 1978, by Wang from 1978 to 1983, and by WordStar from 1983 to 1986, was now ours. WordPerfect for DOS, our cash cow, had again more than doubled in sales.

At our Christmas party, Alan was excited about our growth and optimistic about the future. Looking a lot like a child about to give his mom a Mother's Day present, he offered to take the entire company to Hawaii if sales reached $100 million in 1987. There was no question about whether we would make it—doubling sales every year was easy.

# 8

# GOING TO WAR

We started 1987 with a 30 percent share of the word-processing market, well ahead of Micropro at 16 percent, IBM at 13 percent, and Microsoft at 11 percent. That share represented a tremendous amount of money, enough that we were finally beginning to understand how important WordPerfect was to our future. Instead of trying so hard to shed our one-product image, we now saw a much greater potential if we concentrated on word processing. We were not totally abandoning our other products, but having made it to the top of the word-processing heap, we were going to make sure we stayed there before we went after other markets.

Our new marketing strategy had three parts: first, we wanted to write a version of WordPerfect for every plat-form that made sense; second, we wanted to make sure WordPerfect was well integrated with the other impor-tant products on each platform; and only then did we want to attempt the third part—to create other products for each environment. On the PC, this meant making sure WordPerfect worked well with Lotus 1-2-3 before we worried about making MathPlan a success. On the VAX, this meant having WordPerfect work well with All-in-One before we worried about writing our own electronic mail for the VAX. By focusing our efforts on WordPerfect, we felt we could provide a word processor that would satisfy almost every customer on almost every machine.

This idea varied from the image that a lot of trade publication writers seemed to be promoting. They were writing what I called "Mr. Rogers reviews." Like the song from "Mister Rogers' Neighborhood," which said how fancy and fine everyone was, the reviewers seemed to feel that every word processor had something valuable to offer.

One PC magazine liked to divide word processors into categories for personal, corporate, and professional use, and publish an article on the best products for each category. The personal category was for nonprofessionals and high-level executives—those who did not need a lot of powerful features, who generally had poor typing skills, and whose attention span was too short for them to learn how to use the computer properly. A product like PFS:Write was cheap and more than sufficient for the computer-challenged. The secretary was a typical user in the corporate category. She was described as a "heads-down" user, or someone who spent the entire day sitting at the computer with her head down, looking at the keyboard, typing away like crazy. The standard corporate user needed more features than the personal user, but didn't need all the features of the professional writer. Since she already knew how to use a Wang word processor, Multimate was considered a good enough choice. The professional category was for elite computer users, those with special needs who were knowledgeable enough to use the powerful and complex products like Microsoft Word, WordPerfect, or XyWrite.

This type of analysis made me angry. More than a few nonprofessionals and executives knew how to type and use computers, and I thought a secretary deserved to use the best product available. I felt that anyone who was serious about their writing should be able to use a professional-level product.

I believed a business was much better off finding one word processor that would satisfy everyone rather than a number of word processors to meet individual needs. Documents were not just printed and sent off in the mail—they were passed around, revised, reworked, and published as computer files without ever appearing on paper. To do this easily, an organization needed to have compatible documents in all its departments. Even if an executive never added a footnote to a document, he still needed to read a footnote if the legal department sent him a brief containing one. The legal department may not have wanted to write equations, but if an engineer in another department included one in a patent proposal, then a lawyer's word processor would have to support them.

In addition to having the same word processor used throughout an organization, it helped if the same word processor was used everywhere. If one law firm worked with another on a case, their documents needed to be compatible. If a businesswoman was away from the office, she wanted to find the word processor she used at work on her home computer, her laptop, and at her hotel's business center. If a business needed temporary help, it needed the temporary agency to send someone who already knew how to use its word processor. The world did not need the incompatibilities that came with many different products. The world needed a standard.

WordPerfect was in the best position to become the world's word-processing standard. We were on practically every machine, while Microsoft was only on two of the little ones and IBM was only on IBM's machines. If we could get 5.0 right, we had the potential to stay on top for many years.

Getting WordPerfect 5.0 right was not an easy thing to do, however. Wang had proven a company could lose the number-one spot by moving too slowly. Micropro had proven a company could lose it by moving too quickly. Somehow we had to find a way for 5.0 to support the new technology without making our old customers unhappy. We had to make sure that the improvements in our new product were attractive enough to overcome the resistance our old customers had to installing new releases. If 5.0 was too different, too slow, or required too big of an investment in new hardware or new training, we could get into trouble. Since we knew when we started that WordPerfect would have to be a little different, a little bigger, and a little more complex, we had to be careful.

The initial focus of 5.0 was to improve WordPerfect's printing. The new printing capabilities were designed not only to take advantage of the laser printer, but also to take advantage of any special features built into almost any printer. Our plans for the release were expanded, however, when Dave Moon came to the board shortly after starting his desktop publishing project. He had come to the conclusion that most of what he and his group were planning to do could be included in WordPerfect 5.0. Instead of working on a separate DTP product, Dave wanted his group to add support for graphics into WordPerfect 5.0. Dave believed his group could give WordPerfect users the capability to do 75 percent of what a desktop publishing package could do.

His proposal meant giving up the desktop publishing market, but if we followed his advice, we would jump ahead of what we had heard Microsoft was planning for their next version of Word. We would also be able to offer software that had an obvious advantage over anything available from the dedicated word-processing vendors. And, considering how much trouble we had selling our other products, giving up the market to improve WordPerfect was not a big sacrifice. Dave's suggestion fit right in with our new word-processing strategy, and we told him to go ahead with his plan.

Adding graphics support took no small effort. Integrating text and graphics had been an unrealized dream of word-processing companies for years. To do it right, we had to wrap text around the graphic boxes, and allow the boxes to sometimes stay in the same place on a page and sometimes move with the text. The graphics could take up a lot of disk space, so we had to find ways to accommodate the large files. Since DOS had little support for graphic images, we had to build all the system software pieces to display and edit the figures.

The people in the marketing department went crazy when they heard that graphics support was coming. It would be a lot more fun for them to sell a product that was way ahead of the competition.

Thousands of design decisions had to be made for 5.0. One of the toughest was whether or not to make it a full WYSIWYG product. WYSIWYG, pronounced "wizeewig," stands for "what you see is what you get." This was the ideal situation in word processing: to have the screen—what you see—look exactly like the printed page—what you get. When we started in the word-processing business, WYSIWYG meant showing bold and underlined text, line endings, and page endings on the screen as they would be printed. Of the early PC products, ours was the only one to do this. As time went on, and especially after the introduction of the Macintosh, users wanted a "true" WYSIWYG, with fonts in the same size and style as they were to be printed, with headers, footers, and footnotes in the right places, and with any document illustrations accurately displayed on the screen.

Offering a true WYSIWYG word processor for DOS was not easy. DOS was designed to work in either text mode or graphics mode, but the screen display was much slower in graphics mode. In text mode, the computer handled the screen as if it had twenty-five lines of text, with up to eighty-one characters on a line. When you multiply these two numbers, the answer adds up to only 2,025 boxes on the screen that the program has to worry about. In graphics mode, the computer worked with tiny dots. With the standard 640 times 480 dots for every square inch on the screen, this amounted to literally millions of dots for the computer to address. Since managing millions of dots takes much longer than handling two thousand boxes, the screen display in a graphics mode is much slower.

Another problem was that DOS came with only the barest of essentials for controlling the screen. To control the screen properly for handling fonts and graphics, we either had to write our own screen drivers and come up with our own screen fonts, or try to use Windows, which was designed to to do both, but was still slow and unreliable. Microsoft needed more time, and customers needed faster computers before Windows would be an answer to the WYSIWYG question.

After long discussions about whether to produce a full WYSIWYG version with DOS, we made a compromise. Normal typing would be done, as always, in text mode. The graphics mode would be used only for doing a preview of the printed page and for working with the graphics figures. A print preview was not as good as WYSIWYG editing, but it did give the writer a good sense of how the document would look when printed. This compromise saved us a lot of work and was probably the best solution for the customer until faster machines came along. Full WYSIWYG would have to wait until 6.0.

There were a lot of other new features planned for 5.0, including automatic cross-referencing (if "see page 14" appeared in a document and then three pages were added, "see page 14"automatically changed to "see page 17"); support for more than fifteen hundred characters, including international characters and diacriticals; intelligent printing (if a document designed for one printer was moved to another printer with a different set of fonts, WP would decide which of the new fonts to use and how best to print the document); master documents (many documents could be combined and printed together as one document); bulleted outlines (lists with bullets in front of each item); and automatic redlining and strikeout. There were hundreds of minor features as well.

We were in meetings for a long time, going over what had to be in the product and how things should work. These decisions were made by the programmers, who sometimes had very heated discussions about what was needed, and occasionally, the three of us on the board had to assume the role of referee. Some of the issues were very complicated, and by the time the arguments were finished and a decision was made, I usually had a headache.

It was somewhat unusual for a software company to let the programmers decide the future of its products. We were, however, a company founded and owned by programmers, where programmers were treated with an extra measure of respect. The marketing department primarily sold products once they were developed, and only rarely got involved early enough to perform the traditional marketing role of identifying a need and defining a product to fill that need. Sometimes this put us in the position of developing solutions before we identified problems, but it was hard to be critical of the programmers when the company was so successful. To their credit, the programmers tried to listen to our customers and to those of us in marketing. The programmers were smart and thoughtful and very good at protecting the company's best interests. At times, however, they were apt to manipulate some of the data they received to fit what it was they wanted to do.

Although much of the work we did in 1987 was very

difficult, we did have some fun. At one of our high-level meetings (this was the name we gave to the meetings Alan liked to hold on the ski slopes), we talked about the new laptop computers. As we rode the lifts, we came up with the idea for Executive WordPerfect—a collection of software that included "junior" versions of WordPerfect and MathPlan, along with the calculator, shell, and notebook from Library. The product, conceived in February, was shipped in May. Executive sold fairly well and gave us something new to talk about at the spring COMDEX in Atlanta.

Since we had Micropro on the ropes, we thought we should put them away for good, and we came up with a knockout punch for WordStar that year. We commissioned two editors from one of the best trade publications to write a book entitled *A WordStar User's Survivor's Guide to WordPerfect*. The two writers, who had used WordStar for many years and liked it, wrote the book under the pen names W. P. Forever and W. S. Farewell. Not only was the book funny and useful, but we now had two more press people who knew our product inside and out.

We built an advertising campaign aimed at die-hard WordStar users, offering them the book for a dollar, along with a discount coupon for WordPerfect. We gave most of the copies away for free, because the cost to run a credit card charge through our fulfillment company was more than the dollar we were charging. The only reason we asked for a little money was to scare off those people who didn't really need the book. The campaign was a great success, convincing many diehard WordStar users to finally switch.

By now it had been almost a year since I first tried to write our company's purpose, goals, and objectives. I had had a lot of trouble figuring out the difference between goals and objectives. The dictionary didn't help much, because it used each word as the definition of the other. After agonizing over this for a few months, I finally concluded that a goal was a desired result that you could measure, while an objective was a desired result that was easier to visualize or describe than to measure. By this definition, reaching $100 million in sales or scoring a touchdown were goals, because they involved reaching a particular number or crossing a certain line. Offering the best product or being honest in every business deal were objectives, because there was no number or line involved. Likewise, losing ten pounds would be a goal, but looking good in clothes would be an objective.

I was not sure that it mattered whether I understood these words correctly, but the exercise of trying to understand them helped. I had never liked the idea of assigning a number to every goal or objective. Being "fair and honest" did not have to be translated into "less than fifteen complaints to the Better Business Bureau." "Fair compensation" did not have to be defined as "an employee turnover rate of 4 percent per year or less." "Working hard" did not have to mean reaching a sales goal. I liked using images and what images suggested, rather than precise measurements. If we all had an image or an idea in our minds of what it was we hoped to accomplish, I felt we would have a greater chance of success than if we lived and died by our numbers.

Sometime in the spring, Alan went to a one-day seminar and came back with our mission statement. I was more than a little frustrated with him. I had spent most of a year getting ready to suggest our purpose and objectives, and he had written them down in an afternoon. The definition of our principles seemed so important to me and so central to the proper management of the company that I wanted every word to be perfect.

Alan's mission statement gave me the incentive to finally get moving. I took my work, incorporated many of Alan's ideas, talked to Bruce, and by May published the first version of our purpose and objectives. Our purpose was to develop, market, and support the finest software in the world. Our objectives were to maintain the highest standards of honesty, quality, and service; to maintain a management structure that was efficient and rewarding based on team proficiency; to maintain a quality of life that would encourage employees to stay with the company, keeping turnover to a minimum; and to avoid indebtedness or any public stock offering.

I also put together a long list of policies and procedures, which with our purpose and objectives I called our principles, but I did not pass them around very much. We were still a lawless community of superstars who weren't ready for any serious rules.

In June, we went to PC/Expo knowing Microsoft was going to show Word 4.0 for the first time. We examined the new product very carefully, looking for weaknesses and comparing its features to those we were putting in 5.0. They had improved the speed of the program and added a faster-moving cursor. They had included a WordPerfectlike macro feature with a macro language and a redline/strike-over mode, as well as some file management features and screen options so users could make their Word screens resemble our WordPerfect screen.

After hearing so many rumors for so many months about Microsoft's new product, we were all relieved to see it finally. André summed it up best when he said, "Word is still Word." Though they had some interesting new features, we were in good shape. Their interface was still confusing and their product was still from the old run-off/repagination school of thought.

The best way to understand the difference in our products then was to compare Word and WordPerfect to a magic trick. In our case, we understood that word processing was an illusion. The computer was never designed for writing, and it was only by magic that a computer screen could look like the printed page. In their case, Microsoft seemed to use brute force to get the job done; their columns were inflexible, and they had to use a repagination before printing. Anything fancy had to be done with a style sheet. It was as though they didn't mind letting people "see" how their magic was done. If Microsoft and WordPerfect both performed the old magic trick of sawing a lady in half, we would have been smart enough not to hurt the woman when creating the illusion, but Microsoft would have cut her in half, and then sewed her back together again. Perhaps I overstate our advantages, but not by much. The only time I saw good magic come out of Microsoft was with Excel, its GUI spreadsheet. I hoped for our sake that Excel was merely an accident.

Not everyone in the press shared our impression of Word 4.0, because it received some good reviews. By the end of the summer, we were tired of reading stories about Word's terrific laser printing. We were tired of their promotions, their advertisements, and their slams against WordPerfect. We were tired of hearing they would soon be number one.

On Labor Day, a few of us in marketing were working even though it was a holiday. We went to a long lunch and talked about how fed up we were with Microsoft's claims of a better product. We were in an especially bad mood, because we had recently learned that 5.0 would not be ready for COMDEX in the fall. The release date had been pushed back to February or March, and we were not looking forward to letting Microsoft beat us up for another six months. The longer we talked, the angrier we got, until finally we decided we were going to fight back. We all put our hands together, much like a basketball team at the start of the big game, and made a formal declaration of war against Microsoft. These were desperate times, and we were going to take desperate measures. We would no longer maintain our normal, nice and polite manner, we were going to dispute their false claims, point out their weaknesses, and if necessary, stretch a few rules.

Stretching the rules did not mean doing anything

illegal. It meant we would systematically leak information about 5.0 to the press to build interest in the product. Preannouncing it might hurt our sales a little, but it also might convince potential buyers of Microsoft Word to postpone their purchases until our product was released. This was a little out of character for us, but this was war.

The first step in our battle campaign was to hold a marketing boot camp. For the first time, we had formal training for all home office salespeople. The training stressed teamwork and planning, both of which were necessary if we were to win against Microsoft. For the next few months, each group was to come up with a plan, including a list of objectives and the responsibilities for each person in the group, and get approval for it. Everyone was to know what they were supposed to do, and the plans were to be shared so that everyone would know what everyone else was doing. I stressed that "responsibility was given without autonomy." In other words, everyone was expected to communicate what they were doing with others, so others could offer suggestions and improvements. We were not to be a group of individuals, each working privately and independently; we were a team and we were united against our opponent.

Our second step was to preannounce WordPerfect 5.0. We didn't wait until our product was ready to ship or in a beta test; we starting leaking information right away. Those of us who were traveling started showing it "confidentially" to dealers and large accounts. André showed it to standing-room-only crowds at Softeach, a series of dealer seminars put on by Softsel. I started a series of messages, which I called Bedtime Stories, and posted them each night on CompuServe, an electronic bulletin board, just before I went to sleep. For the next two months, I provided a detailed description of 5.0. At first I revealed very little, giving only the history of WordPerfect Corporation and some of our objectives for the new product. Then, much like a striptease, I revealed

5.0's secrets one at a time. As I introduced each new feature, I explained in detail how it would work. I also asked for suggestions and used the forum to conduct last-minute market research. The stories were monitored by the press and widely republished. They did a great job creating interest in 5.0.

Next, we brought in our thirty-five reps from around the country for a week in October and showed them 5.0. Even though we were still adding features to it, we sent them home with demonstration copies. By early November, all of them would be able to show their customers and dealers what we were showing at COMDEX. We also visited many of the trade publications and gave them preview copies so they could write about it in their special COMDEX issues. The early announcement put a lot more pressure on our programmers to get the product ready and gave Microsoft more time to copy what we were doing, but we felt we had no choice.

Anyone who thinks we might have been overreacting to Microsoft's threat to our future sales has probably never run a business. America's free enterprise system is not designed for the squeamish. It is based on competition and the survival of the fittest. On the surface, capitalism is admirable because it offers everyone an equal opportunity to prosper, but there is an ugly side to it. When many businesses go after the same customer, and especially when some of those businesses are desperate to make a sale, there is a fierceness to the competition that is as frightening and violent as any fight to the death in the jungle. The laws which are supposed to prevent the strong from preying on the weak do not help much. Although competitors are almost always civil and courteous to one another, they are nonetheless at each other's throats.

At COMDEX we held a press conference to formally announce 5.0 and we showed the unfinished product in our booth. André and his staff had put together another amazing show. With the help of our actor friends from

Chicago, they created a classroom for word-processing pilots called Top One. Those attending listened to music from the movie *Top Gun* as they took their seats, put on their Top One hats, and became student pilots. During the show they earned their Top One wings by watching our actor-teachers demonstrate all the new and amazing features in 5.0. In an Officers' Club, we gave special attention to our dealers and large customers. André's work was so good that year that it earned him an award from *Sizzle Magazine* for the best trade show presentation of 1987.

Our Mac group showed their product at COMDEX as well. The programmers were slowly getting rid of its bugs, but their release date was still up in the air. They wanted WPMac to be released before the end of the year, but couldn't make it. At the Christmas party, the Mac developers came with grocery bags over their heads to hide their embarrassment, singing "Waiting for the Macintosh to Ship" to the tune of "Walking in a Winter Wonderland."

While our 5.0 news was big, the biggest news at COMDEX that year was OS/2 and Presentation Manager. IBM and Microsoft had previously announced their intention to collaborate on what was to be the next major PC operating system. Named OS/2, the operating system included the Presentation Manager, which, like Windows, was a platform for GUI applications. For reasons known only to IBM and Microsoft, Presentation Manager and Windows were different, so applications companies like ours had to write two versions of their own products in order to support both platforms.

I participated on an OS/2 panel at the show and was stunned by the audience's feelings about OS/2. Except for a very small minority, everyone there was interested in buying and using OS/2 with the Presentation Manager. There was virtually no interest in applications written for any other operating system, including those written for Windows. No one seemed to have a clear idea about why they wanted OS/2 PM, but they all seemed to

believe there would be many new and wonderful applications and many new computing improvements
resulting from the new operating system. Customers
were expecting the unimaginable.

I felt like an outsider. I had no clue about what the
customers were hoping for, and we were too busy worrying about winning the DOS market to get too excited
about OS/2. It disturbed me to see people so anxiously
anticipating an operating system that was unavailable.
Nevertheless, the race was on for software developers to
come up with the next 1-2-3 or the next application
which would define the new platform and compel customers to buy OS/2 PM.

During the panel, one member of the audience yelled
out, "Don't waste your time on the Amiga," and many
people clapped in agreement. In retrospect, the hecklers
were probably right. We shouldn't have wasted our time
on the Amiga, but we weren't ready to put 50 percent of
our programmers on an OS/2 PM project either. DOS
was going to be an important operating system for a
long time, and many of our other WordPerfect versions
were bringing in significant revenues. We would start
work on OS/2, but we wouldn't drop everything else to
do it.

As we neared the end of the year, it looked like our
sales would be around $97 or $98 million. This was the
worst possible outcome. We were too close to the $100
million goal not to make it, so Bruce and Alan asked the
marketing department to come up with some sales. We
called a few of our distributors and asked them for help,
and as it turned out, they were expecting our calls. They
were hoping that we would be anxious enough to make
the goal to offer them an extra discount or better terms.
We did in fact offer them special terms and, as part of
the deal, asked them to place their orders by telegram.

The telegrams arrived the day of our company party.
As was the custom, Alan, Bruce, and I each spoke for a
few minutes. Alan started his speech by announcing our

current sales. As he talked, we delivered the telegrams to him one by one. With each telegram, he gave the new sales total. When the last telegram was delivered and read, Alan dramatically announced that we had reached our goal. We ended the year with sales of $100,350,000, just enough to send everyone on vacation in the middle of our war with Microsoft.

We ended 1987 with everyone in the company on their feet, cheering, clapping, and screaming, and that is how it should have been. The year was full of firsts. On Softsel's October 26 hot list, we had made it to the top for all personal computer software products, ahead of 1-2-3 and dBase III. Though Microsoft Word was fourth, our WordPerfect network station pack was listed eleventh. Amazingly, Library was listed as number twelve— the first time we had more than one product on the list. We also finished the first of our many new buildings in the research park. Our pretax profit margin was an enviable 33 percent, and we were making enough serious money to pay for the buildings as we built them. It also looked as if we were winning our war with Microsoft.

# 9

# GOING TO HAWAII

Selling over $100 million of software was easy compared
to the trouble we had fulfilling Alan's promise to take
everyone to Hawaii. We had originally planned to ship
5.0 in fall 1987, hoping that by the first of 1988 our
support calls would slow down enough that we could
take the phones off the hook and all go to Hawaii for a
week. If we all went together, we thought we could hold
a few short meetings so the employees would not be
taxed for the total value of the trip. This was a lot of
wishful thinking, however. Version 5.0 was late, and by
now, 4.2's sales had risen to a level where we were taking
four thousand support calls a day.

Plan B was to go not as a group, but separately,
letting everyone go as their schedules became less demanding. For those who wanted to take the trip, we
offered an $1,800 credit with our travel agent, $300 or
$400 cash to cover other expenses, and three extra days
of vacation. Our travel agent negotiated special rates

with the airlines and the hotels, so that the allowance was enough to cover the cost for two people. For those who didn't want to go, we offered a $1,000 bonus instead.

What seemed to us to be a fairly generous travel bonus—which was given in addition to the normal year-end bonus—was not well received by all of our employees. Many were grateful, but there were also many who were unhappy. Some felt cheated because they had to pay taxes on the value of the trip. Some were disappointed that there was only enough money to visit two islands in the seven day period, instead of the three they had had their hearts set on. Some were angry because we asked them to use two of their vacation days. Some wanted to use their own travel agents. Some decided not to go because their babies were due to be born or because they didn't want to pay the taxes. They felt the $1,000 alternative was unfair. Of course, most of the employees who were unhappy thought I was the cause of their frustration. Alan had offered a free trip, and any taxes or limitations had to be my fault.

When the ship date for 5.0 first slipped, the programmers scheduled to ship the product in February and to go to Hawaii in March. The ship date kept slipping, however. Our travel agent had to change their reservations to April, then to May, and finally to June. The rest of the employees also had trouble getting away. The marketing staff was reassuring customers that 5.0 was coming and preparing for the 5.0 roll-out. The support operators were trying to learn 5.0 while still answering all the 4.2 questions. Others in the company were struggling to keep up with the growth in sales and employees.

As much as we wanted to ship the product right away, we couldn't ship it prematurely. It had too many bugs for it to be finished in a few late-night sessions. The programmers and testers were like a weary army on a forced march across a desert, without food or water. We couldn't push them to go faster for fear they would collapse. By now, almost all of the WordPerfect for DOS developers had put their personal lives on hold for close to a year. Their spouses were growing impatient with all the overtime and vacation postponements. We held meetings with the disgruntled family members to reassure them that the product would soon be finished and that the sacrifices being made were worthwhile.

Our offices stayed closed on Sundays, but work continued around the clock during the remainder of the week. During the day and into the evening, the programmers tried to add the last few features and fix bugs. During the late afternoon and long into the night, the testers tried out the new fixes and looked for more bugs. Many of the support operators worked a second shift late at night to help the testers search for bugs. We had pizzas and sandwiches delivered to keep them all going.

The pressure to ship 5.0 increased as each day passed. By preannouncing the product in hopes of preventing Microsoft from stealing our customers, we had created more interest in 5.0 than we had anticipated. We sent out literally thousands of copies early to make up for the delays. Our large accounts wanted it immediately so they could conduct their evaluations and get their support centers up-to-speed. The editors of trade publications demanded review copies, and some threatened us with bad press if we didn't cooperate. Authors trying to write 5.0 books enjoyed the advance copies, but complained because the software was full of bugs and the interface was still changing.

The printer code was the biggest bottleneck to shipment, because until it was completed, we couldn't finish all the new printer drivers. We now supported hundreds of printers in 4.2, including some that were very obscure. Unless we decided to run the risk of having some very angry customers, we had to include all of 4.2's drivers in the new release. Once the drivers were written, we still needed to test them.

We were all short-tempered. The programmers trying to finish the printing code were still finding flaws in parts of their design, and some of their fixes required changes to other parts of the program. The programmers working on these other areas hated to make changes so close to release, and the leaders of the two programming groups did battle in the hallways. Like the discussions in the early design meetings, the arguments were hard to understand and the proposed solutions were very complex. If I asked a simple question like, "What is the difference between a typeface and a font?", one set of programmers was likely to dispute the other's definition. Sometimes a problem had no good solution, and we were forced to accept a solution no one liked.

For example, if a user created a document at work that was designed to print on a laser printer and then took the document home and used a different computer and printer, should WordPerfect automatically reformat the document when it was retrieved? If the user did not want to reformat the document, what would happen if the printer driver from work wasn't available at home? And if the document was reformatted automatically, would the user be notified and given a chance to cancel the reformatting? As I listened to the discussions, I told myself that all the difficulties we were experiencing would eventually give us a competitive advantage. If all of this had been easy, Microsoft would have done it first and left us in the dust.

To add to our pressure, we were offering free updates to anyone who purchased 4.2 after the official 5.0 announcement at COMDEX. We did this to prevent our 4.2 sales from falling in anticipation of the new release. The offer worked, and our sales for both February and March were more than $10 million each month. Unfortunately, the offer was going to cost us $1 million each month we were late.

In March we went to MacWorld. We still didn't have our Mac product ready to ship, but I decided we should sell it anyway. I used a new term, *betaware*, to describe a product offered for sale during its beta testing period.

For $99, the customer received a buggy copy of the software and the promise of a good copy once it was ready. The betaware customers actually received three copies of the software—the betaware copy, the first shipping version, and a third version because the one that we first shipped still had a few too many bugs for us not to release another copy.

On April 4, 1988 we finally sent our Macintosh product out the door, after more than a year of testing. In its first month we shipped more than twenty thousand copies of WordPerfect for the Macintosh, which amounted to sales of almost $3 million. The reviews for the product were less than glowing, however. Most reviewers felt it was patterned too closely after our PC product, and they were right. Our strategy had been to offer a similar word processor across all platforms. Unfortunately, many in the Mac community who were fervently loyal to their machines, did not see file compatibility with the IBM as important, and were offended by the foreign, DOSlike interface. We were more than a little disappointed by this lukewarm reception from the "Macintosh bigots" (as I liked to call them), who thought we were not sufficiently converted to the Mac way of doing things to merit their welcome. Even those Mac users who wanted the similarity were disappointed with the product because it used the DOS 4.1 file format, rather than the 4.2 or 5.0 format. Eventually we would average sales of $1 million per month and capture about 10 percent of the Macintosh word-processing market. This was not too bad, but we had hoped to give Microsoft more of a run for their money.

On Thursday, May 5, 1988, we finally shipped WordPerfect 5.0 for DOS. This time we were determined to have plenty of product for all our distributors, so by Friday afternoon we shipped an enormous number of copies, perhaps as many as one hundred thousand. What should have been a big celebration quickly turned into a wake, however. Within hours of shipping, we found a bug in the installation program.

Just before delivering the final masters to our manufacturing company, the programmers had discovered there wasn't enough room on one of the disks for all the files they had planned to include. They found a couple of files that weren't really necessary to the program, so they left them off the master disks to save space. Because it was such a minor change, no one bothered to retest the disks before delivering the masters. Unfortunately, the installation program hadn't been changed to reflect the missing files, so everyone who ran it—which was everyone who bought the product—got two error messages warning them that two files were missing. The installation program still worked fine, but the warning scared customers into calling us for help.

We tried to recall as many copies as we could, but we had been too efficient shipping them out. We quickly slipped in a new release that corrected the problem, but it was too late. On Monday, May 9, the calls started to trickle in, and by Thursday, the trickle of calls had turned into a flood. On Friday the thirteenth, there were so many people trying to call us that our busy signals brought down the entire AT&T 800 system in the Mountain West. The phones in the Delta Airlines reservation center and the American Express customer service center, both in Salt Lake City, all went dead. AT&T called around lunchtime to politely inquire about when we thought we could clear up our busy signals. Much to our embarrassment, we had no answer for them. We were in deep trouble.

The new release had a few other problems as well. Not all of the printer drivers were ready, and not all had been thoroughly tested, so we had many irate people wondering how they could get their printers to work. We were having trouble with print preview and the graphics editor, features that required a graphics mode. We had assumed, based on representations from manufacturers, that most of the graphics cards on the market would be compatible with those we had tested. After the release of 5.0, however, our customers were finding some incompatibilities we hadn't anticipated.

Looking back, it's difficult for me to blame the programmers or the testers for the problems we had with 5.0. The developers had worked so hard for so long that if we had not shipped when we did, it would have taken us the rest of the summer to recuperate and finish the testing. They had marched across the desert until they dropped and then had kept crawling as far as they could. When they could go no farther, we shipped. Prior to 5.0, our testers had to go a week without discovering any major new bugs before we would ship. The last week before its release, the developers didn't find any new bugs, but by then everyone was so tired that no one wanted to find them. In their defense, most of the problems except for the installation had to do with little-known graphics cards and printers. Perhaps if we had used more customer beta test sites, we could have found more of the incompatibilities.

Though it was hard to believe, customers were buying 5.0—bugs and all. They were angry and disappointed and took many opportunities to chew us out, but they still bought it. WordPerfect 5.0 delivered on almost all of the promises we had made. With a laser printer attached to a PC, 5.0 could print what resembled typeset-quality work. In fact, my neighbor, who sold Macintosh computers for a living, wouldn't believe an IBM PC could print the way a Macintosh could until he saw it with his own eyes.

The reviewers were very kind to us. *InfoWorld* had changed their scoring criteria again, but even with our "Poor" rating for technical support, the 7.9 overall score they gave us was good. The headline read: "New WordPerfect Is Once Again King of the Hill." *PC Week*, which had become an influential publication, was even more complimentary, saying, "This is simply the best

there is in word processing . . . well worth the wait . . .
an all-too-rare software product: one that is genuinely
worth getting excited about."

As soon as the programmers came back from Hawaii
in June, we started fixing our other bugs, and soon were
shipping much cleaner software. That summer we spent
a lot of money sending out free disks to those customers
who had received the flawed early copies. We also visited
customers and spoke at user-group meetings to reassure
people that 5.0 was reliable and that we were doing all
we could to answer the support calls.

I enjoyed visiting the user groups. Practically every
city had at least one, where computer users would meet
to help one another learn to use their computers. Most
of the members were men, but many women attended,
too. Users of all ages came, including quite a few elderly
people. Some members came still wearing their work
clothes but most people dressed casually. A normal meeting consisted of a few announcements, a question-and-
answer period during which people with problems
could ask for help, one or two demonstrations or presentations from computer or software companies, and a
drawing for prizes provided by the presenters.

When I visited a group to make a presentation, I
liked taking questions from the audience. I could count
on a few hecklers who were unhappy about not getting
through to customer support, and I learned to enjoy the
exchanges. I did my best to explain our problems and
what we were doing to fix them. I also dropped a few
hints about upcoming products and explained the reasons behind many of our decisions. I almost always
found that customers were willing to give us time to
correct our problems and mistakes as long as we were
honest and fair with them and tried to do our best.

Fixing customer support was not as easy as fixing
our buggy software. In the short-term, we asked everyone
in the company to take support calls. When customers
couldn't get through on a support line, a lot of them

started calling our other phone numbers. All of us, including Alan and me, tried our best to help these people rather than transferring them back to a busy signal on the support lines. To further relieve the strain, we installed a special 800 number just for installation questions, using trailers as temporary office space and hiring new employees—who read from scripts—to help people get started with 5.0.

Coming up with a long-term solution wasn't easy. Even if the product had been clean, we still wouldn't have had enough people in customer support to handle the needs of our growing customer base. We had simply underestimated everything about 5.0's release. First, we had hired and trained enough people to cover a 25 percent sales increase, but the number of copies we were shipping increased by more than 100 percent. Second, we had not planned on many calls coming in from our old customers buying updates, because our 4.0 customers hadn't needed help with 4.1, nor had our 4.1 customers called when they moved up to 4.2. With 5.0, however, a very high percentage of update customers asked for help. Third, we had expected the average number of minutes per call to remain the same, but we were wrong again. Due to the increased complexity of the software, average call length went from seven minutes to almost fifteen.

Before the release of 5.0, we had 200 operators taking a total of about five thousand calls a day. By August the support staff had grown to 340 operators, but, as a result of the long call times and the inexperience of the new hires, they could handle only six thousand calls a day. Because our sales had doubled, we would have needed to answer at least ten thousand calls a day, even if none of our update customers called us. Three months into 5.0's release, we still weren't close to figuring out how to answer all the calls.

Things were so bad that Dan Lunt actually asked me for help. After almost nine years, Dan and I still had trouble working comfortably together. He had joined the company only three months after I had. When Don left and Bruce and Alan asked him to help me with the marketing, he said he would on the condition that he would work "with" me, but not "for" me. At the time, this condition was not very important in our all-for-one-and-one-for-all organization. Over the years Dan and I developed a friendship of sorts, but he was never one to get very excited about my organizational philosophies. He liked to give his managers the freedom to run their departments the way they wanted to run them.

He picked me up in his black Porsche one weekend afternoon that summer, and as we drove out through the desert west of Utah Lake, he described the problems in customer support. He was most worried about the morale of the group, because even though they were working their hearts out, they couldn't catch up. Some of the experienced operators were leaving, which was unheard of for us, and we were having trouble finding new operators. When we did, we had trouble getting them up-to-speed. He also told me that our completion rate, or the percentage of callers who got through to an operator instead of getting a busy signal, was a discouraging 10 percent.

I discovered that the starting salary for a support operator was only $850 a month, which was probably the biggest reason we were having trouble finding good people. Once trained, the operator was assigned to a supervisor, who was responsible for about seventy-five people. The groups were large because Stan Mackay, the director of the department, was trying to follow my advice and keep a flat structure. The groups, however, were too large for one person to manage, and an unofficial layer of administration had developed to fill in the management gaps. This layer included trainers, who were responsible for the ongoing training of the operators; resource people, who were there to answer tough questions; monitors, who listened in on calls and occasionally graded the operators;

and ICE people, who answered correspondence and kept track of enhancement requests.

Those in charge of the support department, I learned, were busy designing the floor plan for their new building in the research park. In the center of both floors of the building were private offices for the director, his group leaders, and the elite corps of trainers, resource people, monitors, and ICE people. The operators—the unfortunate many—were destined to work in the outer fringes of the building, in small cubicles far away from their leadership.

It was not hard to figure out why morale in the department was so low. Not only were the operators poorly paid, but they were treated as if they were second-class citizens. There were so many of them in each group that they hardly knew their group leaders, and when their work was graded, it was done secretly by monitors who never talked to them face-to-face. Ironically, many of the people we paid to answer phones viewed it as punishment. They couldn't wait for the day when they could leave their headphones behind to join the ranks of the elite, who had already made it off the phones.

Over the next month after our ride in the desert, I helped Dan and Stan reorganize the department. (Of course, the group leaders didn't want smaller groups—they wanted their own assistants so their groups could grow.) Instead, we divided all of support into teams of no more than twenty-three people, each team comprising one team leader and twenty-two operators. We took a few of the old trainers and formed one training group, putting the remaining trainers back on the phones. The ICE people and the monitors also went back on phones, except for a small group assigned to edit the database of support information. Instead of using what I fondly called the Secret Police, we turned the monitoring over to the team leaders.

Another step was the elimination of the private offices in the middle of each floor and their replacement with more cubicles. We gave the team leaders two cubicles each and enclosed their space with glass. By positioning the leaders in the center of their groups and providing them with these semiprivate offices, we hoped that team members would get the attention and help they needed.

We arrived at a team size of twenty-three because the cubicles were originally laid out in groups of twelve. Given the two-cubicle space required for the team leader, we could have had teams of eleven, twenty-three, thirty-five, or forty-seven. I thought at the time that ten operators were too few for one leader and that more than twenty-two would be too many. We eventually learned that it was best to start new team leaders with only ten or twelve operators, letting them work up to twenty-two as they gained experience.

Once we felt we had provided the operators with a means of getting the support they needed, we attended to their low wages. We raised the starting salary for support operators to $1,350 a month and designed a salary schedule that allowed a good operator to move up to $1,800 a month after two years. We hoped the changes would help the operators feel as if their jobs were important and provide incentive for them to stay on the phones.

One of the best changes we made was to limit the number of phone lines going into each group. Operators had been required to spend five-and-a-half hours of an eight-hour shift on the phones. The rest of the day, they were either in training or calling customers back with solutions to the problems they couldn't answer on the first try. Our support lines were open eleven hours a day, from 7:00 A.M. to 6:00 P.M. Mountain Time, in order to cover the hours of 9:00 A.M. to 5:00 P.M. for all time zones in the continental United States. Each team of operators had a specific assignment—for example, answering installation questions or answering network questions— and was responsible for that assignment for the entire eleven-hour period. Because each of the twenty-two team members was on the phone for exactly half of the eleven-hour period, it made sense to limit each group's number of lines to eleven. Dan added a twelfth line so an extra caller could get into the system and wait for a free line. By limiting the number of lines, the number of calls an operator had to face became a finite quantity and our hold times went down.

As we moved into the new building and worked into the new organization and higher salary schedule, morale improved. Gone were the hidden monitors, with their point system for evaluating operators. Gone were the elite positions and the tremendous incentives to get off the phones. Gone were the days when supervisors didn't have the time to meet the needs of their people.

Of course, not everything worked perfectly. For unknown reasons, the trainers decided they should turn their initial operator training into something resembling a military boot camp. I never understood why they took so much pride in making a new operator's first experience with the company so difficult. We also had trouble finding good team leaders. At least one-third of the leaders we tried out weren't strong enough to let their people know when they were doing a poor job. Another third were simply too tough and had trouble treating their team members with respect. They had difficulty understanding that their purpose was to help their team members, not boss them around.

By November, we had hired and trained enough people to begin to handle all the support calls. It had taken us six months to get our completion rates up to a more respectable 50 percent. Except for those times when we seemed to forget that we needed to keep hiring more operators as sales went up, customer support functioned much better over the next few years.

We were focused on word processing, and specifically on WordPerfect for DOS, but we still seemed determined to release as many unsuccessful products as possible. I started telling the old joke about the rancher who won $1 million in a lottery. When asked what he would do with the money, the rancher said, "I'll keep ranching until the last dollar is gone." I felt like we would keep releasing unsuccessful products until our last dollar was gone. We kept planning to put WordPerfect, PlanPerfect, DataPerfect, and WordPerfect Library, which was now called WordPerfect Office, on all important platforms. That some of these products weren't doing well didn't slow us down.

We did have a few successes along with the failures. Surprisingly, WordPerfect 4.2 for DOS kept selling well, because many large corporations decided to take their time about moving to 5.0. Our new WordPerfect Office, with electronic mail for PC networks, and WordPerfect 4.2 versions for UNIX and VAX computers also had good sales. WordPerfect for the Amiga and WordPerfect for the Atari ST started out well, but after only two or three months their sales started to slide. We later tried to boost Amiga sales by releasing WordPerfect Library for the Amiga, but sales were miserable. DataPerfect 2.0 only sold well enough to keep it alive for one more version. Sales for WordPerfect for the IBM 370 (IBM's mainframe) were very disappointing.

Nineteen-eighty-eight was a presidential election year, and for COMDEX, we used Campaign 88 as our theme. With no new version of WordPerfect to introduce and no plans for GUI that we felt we could announce, we chose to have fun. Our press conference was filled with buttons, balloons, speeches, a Dixieland band, and very little substance. We had decisively won our first battles with Microsoft, so we could enjoy our popularity. Our war was far from over, but it was clear that Word for DOS was not a threat.

It was a great feeling to beat Microsoft, because they were a worthy competitor. If you play chess with a three-year-old child and win, it's not as satisfying as beating a grown-up. Microsoft was, in effect, a grand master, which made the game very interesting and the victories gratifying. Bill Gates liked to tell reporters at the fall COMDEX every year that Word would surpass Word-Perfect in the coming year. It was very satisfying to prove him wrong over and over.

We ended 1988 with sales of $178 million, up more than 75 percent from the previous year. Because so many of the packages we shipped were updates, and because we shipped a lot of free copies to correct the DOS and Macintosh bugs, our pretax profits were down to about 25 percent. That amounted to about $25 million after taxes, so we still had more than enough to pay for all the building projects, computers, and furnishings we needed for all our new employees. During the year, we had grown from 554 employees to 1,130, with about half of the new employees going into customer support.

I myself, however, ended the year on a sour note. I broke my ankle four days before the company Christmas party, and having left my temporary cast at home, I was experiencing a fair degree of pain as I hobbled up on the stage to give my short speech. During the previous few weeks, I had received more than my fair share of crank calls and anonymous hate mail, so I was not in a very good mood. When I reached the microphone, I told the employees that I was tired of the complaints and that it was time for all those who were unhappy with their jobs to go somewhere else. It had been a tough year and I was out of patience.

To my surprise, many in the audience applauded my comments. Most of our employees were hard-working and very grateful for the good salaries, the good benefits, and the generous year-end bonuses we provided. They were as tired of the complaining as I was.

If we could have found a way to get rid of all the griping, we would have had the perfect place to work. I wish we could have made it a requirement for all employees to work somewhere else before coming to Word-Perfect Corporation, so they could have understood how lucky they were. If I ever start another business, I will have my employees sign a contract requiring them to come to work with a good attitude. If they decide one day that they don't like their jobs or they don't want to be cheerful, then they will agree in advance to an immediate termination without notice, without severance, and without any accrued vacation pay. Life is too short to spend it with the dissatisfied.

# 10

# SUCCESS

___

Compared to the previous year, 1989 looked easy. We were back in rhythm, planning on another release of WordPerfect for DOS in the fall and expecting sales to rise at least another $100 million or so. Our share of the word-processing market was up to 40 percent and rising. We were in a good position to pull further ahead in the DOS word-processing market, and if IBM and Microsoft fought long enough over OS/2, perhaps we would have time to get ready to win in the GUI market as well.

For the first time, we decided to have a theme for the year, which we introduced at our Christmas party. Having a theme may sound a little old-fashioned or silly, but we took it very seriously. It was a major part of our strategy to increase sales and trounce the competition. After spending more than a year concentrating on our war with Microsoft, we were ready to center our attention on something else.

Our theme for the year was "teach," and we wanted to teach everyone, including our dealers, our customers, the press, and industry analysts, more about using our products. If people visited the office, we were determined to get them in front of a computer and teach them something new about WordPerfect before letting them leave. If we visited customers at their offices, we would try our best to show them something new. If dealers asked for our help on sales calls, we were going to make sure they learned enough to help with the demonstrations. We also wanted all our employees, especially our marketing personnel, to become more proficient with our software.

We received a nice surprise from *InfoWorld* in January. They did a report on the top fourteen word processors and rated the products side-by-side. Although the reviewer had to call our customer support more than once to get through, he eventually got a good answer to his question. Our technical support score improved from a Poor to a Very Good, and our overall score went up to 8.3, the highest of all the products in the review. Microsoft Word 4.0 was given only a 7.0. In printer support, an area where Microsoft at one time could claim a big advantage, we were now rated ahead of Word. Our closest competition was WordStar 2000, but not even a fairly good rating from *InfoWorld* could help sell it. The review slammed Displaywrite with a lowly 4.4 rating. Multimate, now known as Multimate Advantage II, received only a 6.3.

Our 5.0 sales for the year started out strong. Before its release, we had decided not to stress its desktop publishing features in our advertising. We knew we could compete fairly well with the other DTP packages, but felt it wise to promote WordPerfect as the best word processor and let others mention its desktop publishing capabilities. We were worried about scaring customers away by making the product sound too complicated, and the strategy seemed to work well. The press quickly picked up on the DTP features, some even chiding us for not promoting them more than we did. In a *PC Maga-zine* survey conducted early in the year, almost 30 percent of readers planned to purchase their desktop publishing software from us, compared to 38 percent from Aldus, the DTP market leader. This was a great percentage for us considering that we didn't have a true DTP product.

January of 1989 marked the end of our crisis growth era, and we moved the last of the company's departments into the research park. We now had enough money in the bank to plan and build for the future. Soon we added a cafeteria, which Bruce named the Hard Disk Cafe, and a conference center to the complex.

At this same time we were also building a residential subdivision adjacent to the research park. We purchased forty-five acres of an old orchard next door and subdi-vided it into forty home sites. We sold most of the lots at cost to WordPerfect employees and gave them attrac-tive financing. My wife and I purchased a lot right next to WordPerfect's property, just a few hundred feet from customer support. I liked the idea of walking to work and expected to be employed at WordPerfect even when I had to push my walker to the office.

With 5.0's problems behind us, our profits rose back up to the 30 percent level, and we had enough money to start buying out our distributors in Europe. Our inter-national sales were growing, and Bruce believed that a WordPerfect office in each of the European countries would increase sales. We now were the market leader in all the Scandinavian countries as well as Holland and Belgium. Soon we would lead in Great Britain and Spain. We were having only limited success in France, Germany, Austria, and Switzerland, and hoped that a more official presence in Europe would help improve sales in those countries.

In February, per tradition, we invited a few represen-tatives from our largest accounts to come to Deer Valley to ski with us and tell us how we were doing. All of them were concerned about our lack of a WordPerfect for

Presentation Manager, and some of them wanted a Windows version. We tried to reassure them that WordPerfect would eventually run on all important computing environments, and that while we could not always be first to release a product for a new environment, we could catch up quickly. Our large accounts were not too impressed with our answers.

We were having to endure all the OS/2 hype from IBM, Microsoft, and the press, and all the Windows hype from Bill Gates. The Windows programming group at Microsoft had not been disbanded when the company collaborated with IBM on OS/2. Rumor had it that one of the members of the almost-forgotten Windows development team had found a way to make DOS and Windows do much of what OS/2 and PM were going to do. When Scott Oki, vice president of sales for Microsoft, learned that a good version of Windows was possible, he started promoting a Windows strategy rather than an OS/2 strategy to Bill Gates and others at the top. A Windows strategy offered a lot of advantages for Microsoft. If Windows was successful, Microsoft wouldn't have to share control of it with IBM. Even if OS/2 eventually won, it had been delayed so much that Microsoft could still make money selling Windows in the interim. Bill Gates was won over to a Windows strategy and became a one-man Windows promotion team.

Interestingly, early in 1989, Microsoft was still spending more time and money pitching OS/2 than they were pitching Windows, but Windows was now their strategy for the future. Those companies that had significant market shares in the DOS world were quick to see the danger of Windows' success. Most of us threw our influence behind IBM and OS/2, hoping that customers would not fall into Gates's trap. IBM was big, but they were not nearly as dangerous an applications developer as Microsoft. Given the choice of riding on the back of an elephant or a fox, we felt much safer on the elephant.

I became an opponent of Windows out of desperation. I called it a tollbooth on the road to the future. I was irked that many of our customers were willing to buy Windows as an interim solution until the OS/2 Presentation Manager was ready. Not only were they wasting their money, but it created a huge amount of extra work for us to make two GUI versions for IBM PCs. Windows was an ugly piece of software to work with and not an easy platform to support. Even Microsoft had trouble working with it; it took them two years to debug their Windows word processor.

The timing for us was awful. The beta copies of the new version of Windows wouldn't be available to us until early 1990, so we couldn't start work on a Windows product unless we were willing to work with Windows 2.0. Writing for 2.0 meant that we would have to redo much of our work once 3.0 was ready. We were also reluctant to start the project until version 5.1 of Word-Perfect for DOS was finished. We didn't want to release a Windows product that would be one release behind our DOS product, especially since our customers had high expectations about the advantages of a GUI product. We could only hope that IBM would somehow make OS/2 a success; that way, Microsoft wouldn't have too much of an advantage over us in the GUI market.

I took our theme of "teach" seriously. In February I started spending one-half hour each Tuesday morning talking to all the new hires. Some weeks I spoke to twenty or more people. Part of my reason for meeting the new hires was to try to improve my image a little, but I mostly wanted to teach them a little about the company. Many new employees had incredibly high expectations, believing they would have unlimited career opportunities and salaries that would soon grow to enormous levels. I hoped that by talking to them I could bring these unrealistic notions into line with the reality we had to offer.

I explained to the new employees a little of the company's history, its purpose, what we did, and how we were different from other companies. I explained that although we were a wonderful company, our definition of *wonderful* was not necessarily the same as theirs. If, for example, the company chose not to sponsor a little league team, no one should get upset. The purpose, objectives, benefits, salaries, and charities supported by the company were defined by the owners and were sometimes different from what their previous employers might have decided.

I promised the new employees that they would have a good working environment, plenty of meaningful work, good benefits and salaries (although not as high as was rumored around the valley), a board that made careful decisions, and access to anyone in management whenever they had a problem.

In return, I told them, we expected them to work hard, to be reliable and honest, to avoid gossip, and to keep their salaries confidential. The last request was probably asking too much, but we were trying to pay people based on their contribution, and we didn't want them wasting time comparing their salaries. I also encouraged them not to make their job at WordPerfect Corporation the most important thing in their lives. I believed that family and friends should come first, and I didn't want them neglecting their families to get ahead. I was like the drunk who warned others not to drink. I was beginning to recover from my addiction to WordPerfect Corporation and feeling guilty about all the time I had spent away from home over the last nine years. I now believed employees could be more effective if their lives were well-rounded.

I should have explained more about how the company did its work and what employees could expect. Too many people—especially young college graduates with no other job experience—came to work with the wrong expectations and some bad habits. Some couldn't make it to work on time; some couldn't put in a full eight-hour day; some couldn't divorce themselves from their

personal lives once they got to work; and some were
always looking for a ladder to climb and a way to move
past someone else. We didn't need people who were interested in a series of promotions that would help them
reach a goal of fame and fortune. We needed people to
answer phones, to take orders, to keep the networks running, to write software, to test software, and to call on
customers. We specifically tried to avoid those ambitious
individuals seeking "challenging entry-level management positions to improve their interpersonal skills."
We were hoping to find people who would take a job
and do it well, who were not just passing through on
their way to the top. Unfortunately, many people became unhappy once they understood how difficult it was
to move up in our flat organization.

I was also teaching our reps. We now had about one
hundred marketing representatives scattered across the
United States and Canada. Most were young, recently
married, and recently out of college. They were an attractive, hard-working, self-motivated bunch of salespeople
who loved the company and its products, and they were
very different from the poorly equipped and poorly
trained group we sent out the first summer of the program. They were paid a good salary, given good benefits,
and provided with good equipment. They had one
month of training before they went out into the field,
and they were brought back to Utah for more training
twice each year.

I liked getting involved with the reps. When they
published their monthly reports electronically on CompuServe, I always read them and answered many of their
questions. The reps were a good source of information,
because they talked to real customers and knew which of
our marketing programs and strategies were working. I
attended and spoke at their semiannual training meetings and invited their spouses and children to swim in
our pool.

The rep program was something of a case study for

me, where I could test out my management theories and try out new programs, and the sales director who ran the rep program had to put up with a lot of my meddling. Together, we wrote the first rep handbook, which explained the purpose, objectives, and duties of a rep. We experimented with different salary schedules, none of which included a commission, and made sure that the reps were given regular evaluations. We kept the department organization flat. For a time, every one of the more than one hundred reps reported directly to the sales director, who reported directly to me. This proved to be too many reps for one person to supervise, however. We tried using directors out in the field to help supervise them, but the results weren't very good, and we used directors working out of the home office instead.

We tried opening offices in New York and Washington, D.C., and supplying the reps with assistants to see if they would be more effective working out of an office. The offices did little to promote the face-to-face meetings with customers and dealers, which was the purpose of the program, and eventually we closed them, believing the reps were more effective working out of their cars and homes. Offices encouraged activities like staff meetings, paperwork, and telephone tag, and we didn't want our reps sitting behind desks shuffling papers.

We equipped the reps with laptop computers and cellular phones, an 800 number for their dealers and large accounts, and assistants, who worked at our Utah office, to answer the calls, take messages, and schedule appointments. The rep assistants in Utah soon knew the customers in their assigned areas almost as well as someone who had worked in a field office. We saved an enormous amount of money by not opening offices in the major cities.

The rep program had a lean budget, as did the rest of the marketing department. The industry average for marketing expenses for a company our size was about sixteen cents of every sales dollar. We spent only eleven cents. Of those eleven, five cents paid for the customer support phone and personnel costs, leaving us with six cents for marketing salaries, advertising, shows, promotions, and travel. Our competition typically spent only two cents of every dollar on support, leaving them with fourteen cents for everything else. We were very careful about spending money, relying on the strengths of our products and word-of-mouth advertising to do much of our marketing.

As we had expected when we started the year, 1989 followed our normal script closely. Sales went from $57 million for the first quarter to $67 million for the second quarter to $68 million for the third. With 5.1 scheduled for release in the fall, we were set to have another record-breaking year.

Of course, even though overall sales were good, many of our other products were having a tough time. By now the Amiga and Atari products were unprofitable, but we couldn't see an easy way to get out of those markets. Customers who purchased those products and developers who worked on them were extremely loyal to their favorite machines. If we made the slightest move to decrease our development efforts, we made instant enemies. Over the next couple of years we would lose anywhere from $20,000 to $50,000 a month on those two divisions, because we were afraid to abandon even a few of our customers. We were also publishing too many international versions of these low-selling products and manufacturing them in much higher quantities than we could sell. We were, however, having fairly good success with WordPerfect Office for PC networks.

In addition to our Amiga and Atari losses, we were consistently losing money on our Macintosh, IBM 370, and OS/2 groups. The Macintosh group lost money because we were dedicating so many development resources to the next version. Our OS/2 group released a 5.0 non-GUI version, which brought in a little money, but it was not enough to come close to covering the costs

of development of the upcoming GUI product. Our DG
and VAX groups were fairly profitable, but they were
also developing too many products. It gave us some com-
fort to believe that our losers were helping support our
winners. We liked to think that a few Amiga customers
were influencing their employers to choose WordPerfect
as the company standard.

If you counted from the time SSI first incorporated,
we reached our tenth anniversary in September of 1989.
Our PR staff made a big deal of the occasion and we were
recognized quite a bit locally. In addition to the news
stories in the financial sections, it seemed that we received
a new award or special presentation every week. Alan was
Utah's exporter of the year and businessperson of the year
for the local chamber of commerce. Kelly Services made
us their employer of the year in Utah.

Probably the most amazing statistic for those ten
years was our perfect revenue history. For every quarter
during the first ten years we were in business, our collections were higher than the previous quarter. For one
quarter our sales were slightly lower than the previous
quarter, but the money we collected from quarter to
quarter always went up.

In an editorial for the quarterly newsletter that
marked the anniversary, I wrote: "We intend to offer a
complete, integrated, productive, easy-to-use family of
business software products, and we want them to run on
many computing platforms." Looking back, I wish we
had not tried to do so much. Those few customers who
purchased PlanPerfect for the VAX, for example, would
be very disappointed when we stopped development for
that product. We would soon realize that we couldn't
write every product for every machine, and eventually we
would have to cancel some projects, breaking many of
our "family of products on many platforms" promises.
We didn't have the resources to do everything, especially
with our GUI problems.

Rolling out 5.1 should have gone smoothly, but it

didn't. Dan and I had always taken care of the WordPerfect roll-outs, but this time we assigned the work to others. I assumed that the others had watched us long enough to know how to price the updates, come up with a marketing plan, produce the brochures and packaging, get the advertising ready, etc. Of course, we had neglected to provide any formal training for our successors, so as the 5.1 release day approached very little had been prepared.

I realized then that we were still very deficient in our training. When someone was given a new responsibility, I had expected them to do what others had done before them. Instead of learning from previous mistakes, however, the new people always seemed to want to do things on their own, with the same result. We had to live with the blunders, often repeating the same ones over and over again. It seemed to me that in a well-run company, we should not have to let everyone learn by making their own mistakes.

Once Dan and I got involved, the roll-out went smoothly. Dan took care of the advertising, and I wrote a positioning statement. We now had about 60 percent of the word-processing market, so positioning 5.1 as an "all things to all people" product made sense. We stressed that although not everyone needed every new feature, there were a few people in every organization who needed at least a few of the features. The engineering department would like the equations. New users would like the pull-down menus and mouse support. Secretaries would love the tables and labels features. Executives would like the spreadsheet links. Educators would enjoy the larger character set. Someone was sure to get excited about the improved hyphenation, the improved merge, and the more-flexible tabs. Everyone would like the easier installation program. This new major release would result in an entire organization being able to use just one word processor to satisfy all users, even those with very specific requirements.

WordPerfect 5.1 was network-ready right out of the box, so we eliminated our higher-priced network version. Because we were essentially lowering the price of the first network station, we used this as an excuse to raise the price for additional network stations. It made customers upset when we raised the price, but we felt we had to do it. The old $150 price for a computer attached to a network was way too low compared to the $495 price for a computer not attached to a network. Because more customers were now installing networks, we felt we had to raise the price of network stations to avoid a revenue decline.

*PC Week* gave us a lukewarm first review. We now realized that the GUI had taken over the hearts and minds of many of the writers and editors of the trade publications, but we were still surprised to see complaints that WP had "quirky" commands and was difficult to use. It was clear the reviewer didn't like the product, because he wrote, "[WordPerfect] has some things new, some things borrowed (from the competition, that is) and some things old that will leave the users feeling blue." *InfoWorld,* however, was much more complimentary. Their headline, "WordPerfect 5.1 Jumps Ahead of Competition," was all we needed to reassure our customers that 5.1 was a good product.

We celebrated our ten-year anniversary in our COMDEX booth with a seven-foot-tall photo album. As the actors flipped through the pictures, they came to the highlight of our company—the new WordPerfect 5.1. Everything else about COMDEX may have been concerned with either OS/2 or Windows, but 5.1 was a big hit with customers. Sales would jump to $89 million for that last quarter. The tables, labels, and equations were magical, easy to demonstrate, and easy to get excited about. A mob of happy people visited the booth.

Alan and I had lunch at COMDEX with some high-placed officers from IBM. They assured us that Windows would not succeed and that an agreement had been struck between IBM and Microsoft that would effectively stop Microsoft from making a success of Windows. It seems funny now, but at the time we were impressed by what they told us. They said Windows was neutered, and we believed it.

During the COMDEX week, we held a joint press conference with Lotus to announce an alliance of sorts, one in which we agreed to collaborate on our OS/2 products. Lotus had developed a platform that ran on top of OS/2, and they were allowing us to use it without charge if WordPerfect would support it. IBM liked what Lotus was attempting and had given them permission to build links between the new platform and IBM mainframes. By taking advantage of the Lotus platform, we felt we could deliver an OS/2 product earlier while gaining direct access to IBM's large machines and 1-2-3 for OS/2 spreadsheets.

Jim Cannavino, head of IBM's PC division, came and sat in the front row to demonstrate IBM's support for the alliance. We specifically did not invite Microsoft, even though they ached to be involved. In spite of their new Windows maneuvering, Microsoft was still trying to look as though they were leading the way in the promotion of OS/2.

A vice president from Lotus demonstrated 1-2-3 for OS/2. Alan Ashton demonstrated a very fragile, unfinished version of WordPerfect for OS/2, announcing a 1990 release date. Although we weren't ready to announce a firm release date, IBM and Lotus were anxious for us to show our support for OS/2 with some announcement of when we would ship. Jim Manzi announced our Agreement of Cooperation (I persuaded Lotus not to call the relationship an alliance, because I liked Thomas Jefferson's advice about avoiding entangling alliances). I spoke last.

The part I enjoyed most about the whole experience was driving the Lotus public relations department crazy. They wanted to know what I was going to say before the press conference started, afraid I might ruin things and waste the $30,000 we were all spending on the event. They wanted me to give them a transcript of my speech, but I explained to them that I preferred to speak extemporaneously, without a written script. Then they tried to get me to rehearse, but I told them I wasn't prepared. They were accustomed to executives who used the standard speech writer, make-up artist, bodyguard, and publicist entourage, and they didn't know what to do with someone who didn't want all their help. To further tease them, I made sure they saw me writing my speech on an envelope as Jim Manzi made his comments, just moments before I walked on stage.

Of course, I thought I did a good job. I have always loved to get up in front of people, to get their attention, to hold it, and to make them laugh. I made sure everyone knew we were not "getting into bed" with Lotus. This would have been out of character for a company from Utah. Jim Manzi said we were dating, but I tried to make it clear that we were just good friends. Much like two fathers-to-be who struck up a conversation in the maternity waiting room, we had become friends while waiting for our OS/2 babies to be born.

The friendship didn't last very long, however. Microsoft would embarrass IBM greatly by making Windows a very capable product and putting more work into their Windows applications. The Lotus platform, which looked so attractive to our programmers in the fall, would not look as good to them by the next spring. Soon Lotus would acquire a word processor called Amí Pro and become our direct competitor. Our first attempt at having an OS/2 baby would eventually abort, and their first version would be a sickly thing, never amounting to much.

At COMDEX, *Computer Reseller News* always published its list of the twenty-five most influential computer industry executives. I had appeared on their list for the last two years, but this time I disappeared from its ranks. They had called to tell me I would be on the list and to get a quote, but I suggested they put Alan on the list instead. I was a little embarrassed about making the list when Alan and Bruce did not. I was always trying to explain that the three of us ran the company together, but I usually received more of the industry press attention because I went to more industry conferences. Although Alan was considered the chief executive officer in Utah, and Bruce the chief executive officer in Europe, I was generally thought to be in charge everywhere else. No one wanted to believe that the three of us ran the company together, which became apparent when, despite my suggestion, Alan failed to make the Top 25 list.

I was particularly proud of one promotion we came up with for the 5.1 release. We offered to let 5.1 update customers donate their old copies of 5.0 to their favorite elementary, junior high, or high school. The offer required some paperwork, which gave us a chance to identify schools that were interested in using our products. The donations saved schools a lot of money and allowed them to use fairly up-to-date software. The program cost us almost nothing and convinced many more schools to use our products. The part I liked most about the promotion was that Microsoft could not duplicate it. Their installed base of Word users was so much smaller than ours that a similar program would have had very little effect.

We ended the year in great shape financially, with sales of $281 million and pretax profits back up in the 33 percent range. Version 5.1 was a great product and selling very well. We were a little disappointed, however, that the technical advances in the product were largely ignored because of all the attention paid to GUI. The focus of the industry was directed toward Windows and OS/2. Although we were having trouble delivering our OS/2 baby, our employees were having great successes on their own. That year, 222 real babies were born, which was more than one for every eight of our 1,612 employees.

# 11

# BACK TO SCHOOL

———

After the discouraging experience of letting someone else try to roll-out 5.1, I knew it was time for some serious management training. Alan and I, and Bruce to a lesser extent, claimed that our management approach was defined by the statement "We teach correct principles and our employees govern themselves." We borrowed the statement from Joseph Smith, Jr., the founder of the Mormon church, who said "I teach them correct principles, and they govern themselves," when asked to explain how the church was governed. We had attempted to follow this philosophy, but over the years we had not done a very good job of teaching correct principles. Our company was run with a philosophy closer to "We let employees govern themselves, and when they make a mistake, we try to correct them." I was hoping to change this by defining and teaching the correct principles of WordPerfect Corporation in a series of lectures for all managers in the company, lectures which represented the sum of all I had learned over the years.

For practically every week from December of 1989 through mid-1990, I invited sixteen managers to have lunch with me for three consecutive days starting on Tuesday. After lunch each day, I spoke for about an hour and a half. In addition to the managers from WordPerfect Corporation, I held classes for most of the managers from SoftCopy, our manufacturing company; WordPerfect Publishing, the publishers of *WordPerfect, The Magazine;* Computershow, a computer store we owned in Orem; and ABP Development, the company we had formed to construct our buildings. A few of the managers from our WordPerfect companies around the world also attended the lectures.

My approach was low-key. I dressed casually and drank an extra-large Dr. Pepper to keep my throat from going dry (I have since given up both sugar and caffeine). There were no tests and no study materials. No one was forced to come, and no one had to take notes. Everyone was allowed to ask questions at any time and to disagree with anything I said. Instead of telling people what to do, I was trying to convince them that the principles I was teaching were the ones we should follow.

The lectures were an unusual experience for a lot of people. For years, I was the person most feared in the company. When I walked down a hallway, I became accustomed to hearing the sound of desk drawers closing as people hid their snacks from view. When I attended a meeting, it also seemed that at least a few of the people there were afraid to speak to me, unlike Alan, who was welcomed, or Bruce, who usually went unrecognized. By starting with lunch, I was hoping to put people at ease.

The first lecture was mostly a recounting of the history of WordPerfect Corporation. A lot had been written about the company in the trade publications, but many of the newer employees had only a few pieces of the puzzle. By now the three of us on the board were something of a cross between legend and caricature, typecast as the eccentric, the good guy, and the bad guy. I wanted people to see us more realistically, as normal people from relatively modest backgrounds, who worked hard once they found themselves in the right place at the right time. I wanted to explain how I came to believe what I believed. Luckily, none of the history was very controversial, and it served as a comfortable introduction for some of the more difficult-to-swallow material that was to come.

Near the end of the first lecture, I explained what WordPerfect Corporation was not. This set the stage for the next two days, when I would explain what WordPerfect Corporation was.

WordPerfect Corporation was not a platform for personal achievement, a career ladder to other opportunities, or a challenging opportunity for personal improvement. The company did not put the needs of the individual ahead of its own. The company was not concerned about an employee's personal feelings, except as they related to the company's well-being.

WordPerfect Corporation was not intended to be a social club for the unproductive. While other companies might condone many personal or social activities at the office, ours did not. Things like celebrating birthdays, throwing baby showers, collecting for gifts, selling Tupperware or Avon, managing sports tournaments, running betting pools, calling home to keep a romance alive or hand out chores to the children, gossiping or flirting with coworkers, getting a haircut, going to a medical or dental appointment, running to the cafeteria for a snack, coming in a little late or leaving a little early, taking Friday afternoon off, and griping about working conditions were all inappropriate when done on company time. Even though these activities were allowed by many businesses across the country, we felt there was no time for them at WordPerfect Corporation.

WordPerfect Corporation was also not an arena for political games. A good-old-boy network method of trading favors inside the company to get things done was frowned upon. Kissing-up, back-stabbing, and seeking power and position were inappropriate. Making decisions by compromise—the politician's favorite tool— was not acceptable.

Finally, WordPerfect Corporation was not a "New Age" company. We were neither employee-owned nor a democracy. We were not primarily interested in focusing all our attention on either the employee or the customer. We did not feel it appropriate to check an employee's body fat or prescribe a diet or exercise program. We were not trying to stay in step with current business philosophies.

This information, coming all at once at the end of the first day, shocked and upset a few people. No one left without feeling a little offended, which was part of the desired effect. I wanted the participants to question some of their assumptions about their jobs and their company. I frankly couldn't understand how businesses could expect to get anything done when the workplace was turned into a social club. I felt a job was about work, and the personal, political, and social aspects were important only when they were important to the welfare of the company. I certainly was happy if employees enjoyed their work, but I wanted them to understand that their enjoyment and fulfillment were not the ultimate focus of WordPerfect Corporation.

On the second and third days, I did my best to explain the principles that I hoped governed our work at WordPerfect. For many, this was new information, because we didn't have a company organizational chart, an employee handbook, any written job descriptions other than those written for the reps, or a widely published mission statement. How the company was supposed to work was a mystery to most employees.

The principles, as I defined them, included our purpose and objectives and a description of our form and function. The purpose of the company answered the question, Why does the company exist? The objectives answered the question, What does the company hope to accomplish? The form of the company described who went where in the organization. "Function" described the policies and procedures used to define how the company went about doing its work. I didn't believe that this why, what, who, where, how method of defining the company's principles was the only way, but it seemed to be a good framework for our discussions.

Our purpose was to write, sell, and support the finest software in the world. It was not to make huge piles of money or to grow in order to provide continuing opportunities for employees or to raise money to help teenagers say no to drugs. While all of these other purposes were perfectly fine, our reason for existence was to provide the world with great software.

Our objectives were to conduct business fairly, honestly, profitably, and cheerfully, while avoiding debt and extravagance; to maintain an efficient nonbureaucratic organization based upon teamwork, honest and frequent communication, careful and thoughtful decisions; to provide employees with meaningful work, fair compensation, and all necessary assistance for them to do their best work; to develop useful, reliable, and wonderful software products; to market our products effectively, professionally, truthfully, and with excitement; and to offer excellent support for our products.

These objectives were not carved in stone. Bruce and Alan were fairly comfortable with them, but we were still making a few changes. There was some discussion that we should limit ourselves to business software, to emphasize our focus on word processing. The objectives reflected our beliefs enough for me to use them in discussions. Alan did come to two of the lectures and seemed to approve of what I was saying, but he was hard to read, because he was always so agreeable.

The form I envisioned for the company was probably the most difficult part for everyone to accept. In my mind, I saw three groups of people in the company. The first group, the board of directors, defined and published the principles, made the major decisions affecting the direction of the company, and defined the basics of what everyone was to do.

The second group, whom I called the advisors, was responsible for training, supporting, and evaluating the company's employees. I intentionally avoided the word *supervisor*, because I didn't want anyone bossing anyone else around. The advisors were expected to treat the employees who reported to them with respect and kindness. They were expected to let employees know very clearly when they made mistakes and then help them improve their performance. Advisors were not allowed to be overbearing, disrespectful, or unfair. They were expected to care about their employees and not care too much about their company title or position. Advisors were expected to give each of their employees a written job description containing the job's purpose and objectives and to conduct regular performance evaluations based on those job descriptions.

The third group I called managers, and it was composed of the remainder of the employees, all of whom had responsibilities to fulfill or manage. I liked the idea of calling everyone in the company a manager. I wanted every employee to feel like their duties were important. In an ideal situation, the duties of all managers would support the purpose and objectives of the company.

The concept of an advisor left many thinking I had lost my mind, so I spent the last half hour of the second day reading from Peter Drucker's book, *The Practice of Management.* I read Chapter 12, "Managers Must Manage," from beginning to end to prove to them that these concepts weren't completely off-the-wall. This chapter, published in 1954, explained better than anything I had read what it was I was trying to say.

Drucker wrote that "The manager should be directed and controlled by the objectives of performance rather than by his boss. . . . If the manager is, however, controlled by the objective requirements of his own job and measured by his results, there is no need for the kind of supervision that consists of telling a subordinate what to do and then making sure that he does it."

He added: "If a one-word definition of this downward relationship [between a manager and a subordinate] be needed, 'assistance' would come closest. . . . The vision of a manager should always be upward—toward the enterprise as a whole. But his responsibility runs downward as well—to the managers on his team. That his relationship toward them be clearly understood as a duty rather than as supervision is perhaps the central requirement for organizing the manager's job effectively."

I believed what Drucker wrote. The advisors were there to assist the employees, not to tell them what to do every minute or keep track of their every move. An advisor was a teacher, not an overbearing supervisor. Managers should be controlled by their jobs' objectives, rather than over-the-shoulder instructions from a supervisor. The job of an advisor was a duty and not an opportunity to wield personal power.

On the last afternoon, I explained how I thought the company should function, which was the hardest part of all. I could have written out every policy and procedure, but I was much more interested in teaching a few requirements for governing actions and decisions.

The first requirement was that we worked as a team, and I told the story of how two students each approached a college exam to make my point. The first student took the exam without looking at notes or books and without getting help from anyone during the test. This person was very smart and managed to get a fairly good grade, but he didn't get the highest grade in the class. The second student talked to the professor before the exam and learned that she could bring notes and books to the test, discuss possible answers with other students, and ask the professor for help during the exam if she had trouble. The second student received the highest grade, which was a perfect score.

Unfortunately, a lot of people in business are like the first student. They work alone and make decisions alone, perhaps so they can claim all the credit if they succeed. Employees could be much more successful, however, if they followed the example of the second student, who was smart enough to ask for help, and I wanted all our employees to work this way. I hoped they would go to coworkers for suggestions, make use of any information available, and consult with their advisors and other experts around the company as needed. Our work was not a personal effort to gain acclaim—it was a team effort, and we all helped one another so we could all do our best work.

We also needed to communicate freely and frequently. In many companies, it was common for supervisors to keep information to themselves, conceal their mistakes whenever possible, and never allow subordinates to go over their heads. I wanted a company where information could flow freely, with no regard for formal lines of communication. I imagined a room filled with light, without any portion remaining in darkness. I wanted a company in which there were no secrets— where everything was out in the open. Advisors who wanted their employees to be so loyal that they would take their problems only to them were exactly the ones I wanted to kick out of the company. Any loyalty should be directed toward the company's purpose and objectives, not to individual advisors. Advisors who didn't want the light to shine throughout their domains didn't deserve their positions. If employees made mistakes, then the mistakes needed to be admitted so they could be corrected and avoided in the future. I wanted a company where employees could make mistakes, admit them freely, and learn how to do better without fearing for their jobs.

I emphasized planning as the third requirement, and

part of planning was to count costs, always. We wasted a lot of money by neglecting this principle over the years. For example, the 4.2 workbook cost us about $2.30 each to produce. The 5.0 workbook, which had only a few more pages, cost us over $7.00 each. Who approved the increase? No one. One person in publications thought we needed better paper. Another thought we needed more color. A third didn't think we really needed to get three production bids. A fourth thought we needed a better cover. We were shipping 150,000 workbooks every month and spending $675,000 a month more than was necessary. We were wasting more than double the amount we were spending on salaries for the entire publications department.

As the fourth requirement, I asked employees to listen to their hearts as well as their minds. I wasn't asking people to make emotional decisions, but I did want them to listen to their feelings—especially their misgivings and their second thoughts—before they made their decisions.

Alan, Bruce, and I relied on our feelings a lot. It would drive some people crazy to have us change our minds after sleeping on a decision, but over the years we had learned to be careful if we had second thoughts. Our misgivings and impressions, although subjective, generally came from some objective information that had been noted but not thoroughly considered. If we took the time to understand why we felt badly about something, we almost always found a good reason and a better course of action.

People rely on their feelings all the time in nonbusiness settings. When looking for an apartment, clothes, or someone to marry, we make our decisions based on our feelings. Many times, we know we don't like something before we know why. If we examine our feelings closely, we can usually discover what makes us feel a certain way. It often simply takes time for us to figure out that the reason we didn't want to rent a certain apartment was because of the yellow linoleum in the kitchen or the small windows in the bedroom.

If we rely on feelings to make personal decisions, I don't see why they can't be used to help us make business decisions as well. Once, an attorney friend from New York City asked me for advice. He worked for a law firm near Rockefeller Center and was considering taking a job in the Wall Street area. I suggested he take a day off and pretend to go to work for the new company—that he take the subway he would take if he accepted the job, walk to the new office building, and go up the elevator to the floor where he was likely to work. Then I wanted him to ask himself how he felt about the new opportunity. He took my advice, and as soon as he walked out of the subway exit on his way to the new office, he knew he did not want the job. He remembered how much more he enjoyed working near Central Park.

I especially wanted people to consider their feelings when hiring employees. I got very discouraged by those advisors who made it a point not to let their feelings play a part in their decisions. While I didn't want anyone making quick decisions based only on first impressions, I did want people to consider how they felt about the applicants in addition to the applicants' qualifications. If they disliked someone, they should try to figure out the reasons for the dislike and eliminate the misgivings before offering them a job. Once they understood the reasons for the negative feelings, they could make a more objective determination.

The last requirement was that we should all work to avoid bureaucracy, including any unnecessary meetings, any meetings that were longer than necessary, and any unnecessary reports. If all employees learned their duties and governed their own actions based on correct principles, then many meetings and most written reports could be avoided. People should certainly talk and share ideas, but not in three-hour meetings with twenty-five people. I especially disliked the Monday morning staff meeting.

I thought it was ridiculous to tie people up in a meeting when the telephone lines were overflowing with calls from customers who had waited all weekend to talk to us.

I promised everyone in the classes that if they fulfilled these five requirements when they made their decisions, they would not get in trouble with me if something went wrong. They would, however, get into a lot of trouble if they worked entirely on their own with their own agenda, even if their work was good. A decision was correct only if it was consistent with the corporation's purpose and objectives and with how the company was supposed to function.

I knew I wasn't giving advisors a complete picture, but I hoped I was giving them enough to do a good job. If we could work together, communicate openly, plan carefully, listen to our hearts as well as our minds, and avoid bureaucracy, then I was sure we could do a good job for ourselves and our customers. If everyone knew the purpose and objectives of their job and worked to fulfill the purpose and objectives of the company, we could accomplish anything. We could take on Microsoft or anybody else and win if we would set aside our personal agendas and work together.

Of course, not everyone agreed with what I was teaching. Some classes ended in heated discussions. A lot of the advisors didn't like having to be nice to people. They enjoyed being bosses. The most controversial idea presented was that any employee could and should be able to talk to anyone else in the company, including members of the board. Many advisors wanted lines of communication strictly enforced so they would never look bad to their own advisors. Many didn't want to bother the board with little problems. I didn't want the board to be bothered with little problems either, but I also didn't want to prevent people from approaching us with big problems. I had a hard time sympathizing with those who wanted to keep a tight reign on the people they advised. I could not understand why anyone would *want* to be hard-nosed and difficult. I may have been difficult and ill-tempered at times, but at least I regretted it.

The lectures left many holes that still needed filling. After the training was over, I met with advisors, discussing how to write job descriptions, how to perform evaluations, how to set salaries, and how to handle employees if they refused to improve their work. I didn't have all the answers, but I felt we were moving in the right direction. If nothing else, after the training a lot more employees had something in writing that explained what they were supposed to be doing.

# 12

# PROSPERITY

The "teach" theme helped us do a better job promoting our products, but it also pointed out one of our weaknesses. We were great at giving presentations, but we were not very good at listening. Our reps had turned into demonstration machines, some committing what I thought was the worst presentation sin of all—asking customers to hold their questions until the end of the presentation. "Listen" would be the theme for 1990. We would continue to teach, but we would also pay attention to what our customers wanted to learn.

Microsoft offered to make us a beta test site for Windows 3.0 in January. We accepted their generous offer, but did little more than look Windows over. In hindsight, it's easy to see that we should have done much more immediately. We justified not doing a Windows 2.0 version at the time so we could complete WordPerfect 5.1 for DOS, but it was difficult to defend our further delays. Unfortunately, we didn't have any experienced

Windows programmers in the company to form a development team, and there weren't many outside the company to recruit.

Some of us were ready to postpone OS/2 in favor of Windows, but the programmers in the OS/2 group—who had also been assigned to create the Windows version—weren't ready to give up on OS/2. They were making good progress and hated the idea of starting over or splitting their development team into two groups. They wanted to believe in IBM, as did the rest of us: The failure of OS/2 meant having to play on a field owned and operated by Microsoft, with Microsoft making the rules.

We tried to help OS/2 succeed as much as we could. Alan Ashton and André toured the country with IBM, visiting their largest customers and reassuring them that OS/2 was the one and only true operating system of the future. We took every opportunity to show support for OS/2 at industry events, in our quarterly newsletter to customers, and in comments to the press.

About this time, Egghead Discount Software, a chain of two hundred software stores, asked me to drop by their office in Issaquah, Washington. It was one of those occasions when a customer pulled our chain to see if we were properly obedient, and large companies like Ford did it frequently. Ford wanted a president or vice president to show up, making a formal demonstration of devotion and consideration. A good product and good service were not enough. In addition, since Bill Gates himself was visiting Ford to tell them how stupid they were to buy our products, the least we could do was to show an equal amount of concern for the relationship. Because Egghead sent us a check for a few million dollars each month, we had to answer their tug.

I was not the only person invited to Issaquah. Jim Manzi from Lotus was there; Gordon Eubanks, chief executive officer of Symantec, was there; a president or vice president from almost every other software company was there. Egghead had pulled everyone's chain at once, and we all obediently came running.

Victor Alhadeff, president and founder of Egghead Discount Software, was our host. The theme of his speech was a request we had heard continuously from our dealers and distributors over the years. Sometimes the plea was in the form of a blatant threat, as was Businessland's practice. Sometimes it was merely a cry for help. In every case, the dealer was hoping to get special pricing. Every reseller wanted a price that was better than the competition's, and all had a good reason for justifying their special breaks. Businessland demanded better pricing because it offered its customers more services. If they didn't get a price break, they tried every way possible to avoid selling a product. Not surprisingly, no one in the industry grieved much when Businessland failed. Tandy believed it had to have a certain gross profit margin before carrying a product. If other dealers generally discounted a product, which was the case with all of the popular software, Tandy expected the software manufacturer to give them an extra discount to keep their hallowed margin intact. If a vendor refused, its products didn't appear on Tandy's shelves.

President Alhadeff made it clear that Egghead was in trouble. He complained of low profit margins, which was ironic—for years, Egghead had been one of the dealers most responsible for the deep discounts on software. As part of his plea for help, he took us on a tour of his facility, hoping to demonstrate why he deserved an extra discount. He was very proud of the seventy-five programmers he had writing accounting software for the IBM AS/400 (the AS/400 was IBM's new midsize computer, smaller than a mainframe, but larger than a personal computer). Seeing more programmers working on Egghead's accounting software than we had working on WordPerfect for DOS was proof enough that Egghead was having trouble. Mr. Alhadeff's appeal brought him a lot of sympathetic looks, but no special favors. By now, we had all learned from experience the inevitable bad effects of special pricing. Soon after this, there was a reorganization at Egghead, and Mr. Alhadeff was gone.

During the calm before the Windows storm, we released a new product. Once the original desktop publishing team had finished putting graphics capabilities into WordPerfect 5.0, they wanted to continue working with graphics. They wanted to produce software that would make visual aids for presentations, or as it is called in the industry, a business presentation graphics package. The marketing department had been forewarned about the release of the product, called DrawPerfect, but its ship date kept slipping. When DrawPerfect was finally ready in February, we in marketing were taken by surprise. We had a product ready to ship, but no advertising.

The surprise appearance of DrawPerfect helped us pull off our most effective product roll-out. Our usual style was to place ads early in anticipation of a ship date. Later, the ship date would slip, and the ads would be too early. By the time the product was actually ready, our dealers were frustrated with us, because we were sending customers into stores to buy a product that wasn't available. With DrawPerfect, however, our reps delivered a demonstration copy to dealers long before the customers knew the product was being released. By the time our advertising came out, dealers had ordered and received real product for their shelves.

Even though DrawPerfect was a DOS product in a world anxiously awaiting Windows products, it sold well. For the first time in the company's history, we had three products—WordPerfect for DOS, WordPerfect Office for PC networks, and DrawPerfect for DOS—selling more than $1 million a month each.

In the spring of 1990 we implemented what was lauded as one of our most effective innovations—the hold jockey. We now had about six hundred operators in customer support, divided into approximately twenty-five teams, but we were having trouble distributing calls to the various teams. Rather than giving each team a different assignment, we had groups of teams covering the same areas. For example, we had a group of six teams taking questions for general features, a group of five teams answering printer questions, and a group of three teams covering network questions. The telephone system we used wasn't always capable of distributing the calls evenly to each team in a group. While in theory each team was only supposed to have twelve incoming lines, sometimes fifteen incoming calls would go to one team and only nine to another.

One answer was to purchase better equipment. We had been buying our phone system from Rolm at a cost of about $2,500 per operator. If we moved up to better equipment, we would have to throw out the old system and replace it with one that would cost us about $5,000 per operator, or about $3 million for the six hundred customer support employees.

At a meeting to discuss the purchase, I asked if it was possible to have a real person watch the support screens and transfer callers from one group to another when necessary. I thought that having someone with real intelligence would be a much cheaper solution than a new phone system with artificial intelligence. As we discussed the idea further, we decided that this person could also select and play the hold music, do live commercials for our products, provide "traffic" reports (information about wait times on the hold lines), and offer ski reports in the winter.

While we weren't sure we were the first to invent and use live hold jockeys, the program did get us a lot of attention. A number of television and radio stations ran stories about our innovative approach to hold music. Not only did we offer a more personal service to our customers, but the interest that accrued on the $3 million we didn't spend on the new system was more than enough to fund the program.

Microsoft shipped Windows 3.0 in May, and our worst fears became a reality. Just when we were winning decisively in the DOS word-processing market, the personal computing world wanted Windows, bugs and all. To make matters worse, Microsoft Word for Windows was already on dealer shelves and had received good reviews. That little cloud on the horizon that looked so harmless in 1986 was all around us now, looking ominous and threatening. IBM's strength and size were no protection. Not even an elephant could protect us from the impending storm.

May 31, 1990 was a sad day in WordPerfect Corporation's history. I wrote a press release that announced the postponement of our OS/2 product, and our increased emphasis on a Windows version of WordPerfect. The release stated that, "While we still are strong supporters of OS/2, we have decided to test and release the Windows version of WordPerfect before the OS/2 version. The reasons for the schedule change have to do with the expected delays in version 2.0 of Presentation Manager and particular requests from our customers. This change should move up the release of our Windows product by three to four months and will delay our release of a PM product by four or five months."

We had few friends that day. IBM's best large accounts did not understand how much trouble OS/2 was in and were upset at us for breaking ranks. The customers at the other end of the spectrum—those who were Windows supporters—were quick to fault us for our tardiness and tell us "I told you so."

We had been saying that our OS/2 product would be ready for fall COMDEX and that a Windows version would appear six months later. Using these dates, my memo suggested that the Windows product would be available as early as February of 1991 and that the OS/2 product would be ready in May of 1991. The dates would prove to be far too optimistic, however. The Windows product would not ship until much later in the year, and a GUI-based OS/2 product would not ship until 1993.

Ironically, even though we were in trouble, our sales were up more than 80 percent over 1989, and we were making a lot of money. We were doing so well that a few of our DOS programmers couldn't understand why others in the company were panicked. DOS was still king, and 5.1 was raking in 70 percent of personal computer word-processing sales. Though Windows was selling well, Windows-based word processors were not. It appeared that most customers were willing to wait for a Windows version of WordPerfect before buying another company's product.

I'm not sure why Microsoft had so much trouble selling its Windows word processor. Perhaps it was because Windows was still a novelty and customers were content to play with it rather than use it full-time. Perhaps it was because many people didn't enjoy doing business with Microsoft. The company was so driven to dominate the computer industry that its employees came across as overly serious and arrogant. They were almost always giving nerds a bad reputation.

Our technical support was one reason we enjoyed strong customer loyalty to our products. We offered our customers toll-free support lines and tried our best to answer all questions. We felt a real responsibility to help them if they had problems with our software. Microsoft had much more money and resources than we did, and their software had at least as many problems as ours, yet they never put in toll-free lines. Moreover, when they answered their phones, they tended to sound surly. In keeping with their slogan of "making things make sense," they were quick to give the impression that they knew all the answers.

I loved to go to user groups when Microsoft was there. A favorite format of many user-group meetings was to bring two competing products together and have a debate, or a "shoot-out." I liked the format, because I could use humor to get the crowd on my side. Microsoft's representatives were generally too serious to appreciate the humor and were easily rattled if I pointed a joke at them. They also seemed a little too competitive and a little mean-spirited.

In June, as in years past, we went to PC/Expo in New York City. Despite our great sales, the press was already writing our obituary. Everyone at the show asked when our Windows product, WPwin, would be ready—even customers who had no plans to buy Windows. (WPwin was the official abbreviation for WordPerfect for Windows. Alan insisted that we not capitalize the "win" part of the name so as not to emphasize Windows.)

The only bright spot for me at PC/Expo was our introduction of LetterPerfect—our newest, smaller version of WordPerfect. Sam and Wendy, my oldest children, came with me to New York and participated in our press conference announcing it. We explained the product with a little skit. Sam was an experienced word-processor user who wanted the most powerful product, so he needed WordPerfect. Wendy was a young woman too busy to learn all the ins and outs of a complex word processor, so she preferred LetterPerfect. I played the part of the serious writer who required the larger program to meet his word-processing needs. Clive Winn, vice president of sales, played the part of a busy executive who wanted the smaller, quicker product for his laptop. The skit was fun and gave us something to talk about other than our uncertain WPwin release date.

It was not uncommon for my kids to accompany me on my business travels. On those trips that didn't require me to work very many hours, I would take two or three of them along to keep me company. This was only one example of how my personal life blended into my business life. We now lived right next door to the research park, and our home was like another building in the WordPerfect complex. Our phones and our computers were tied into those of WPCorp, so I could work at home or at the office using the same phone number and the same network name and password. This was a great convenience for someone who never wanted to stop working, although it was embarrassing one morning when everyone at WP heard my son Joe yelling, "Mom, the phone is for you" over the company public-address system. (He had dialed in the wrong zone number.) Even our television reception came from a WPCorp antenna.

Most of my friends and a lot of my neighbors and relatives worked at WPCorp. When I went to lunch, it was with friends from work and the conversations were mostly about work. When I played tennis in the late afternoon, it was with friends from work and the conversations were mostly about work. When my wife and I went out to dinner with another couple, the other couple was usually connected to WPCorp in some way. If my wife and I went to New York City for a vacation, I would always fit in a few visits to large accounts. If we had a family reunion, there would always be three or four of us from WPCorp, and conversations would inevitably turn to the company or the software industry. If I watched TV or went to a Jazz basketball game, I always kept something business-related to read during breaks. When the entire family went on vacation, I would have my mail delivered daily to the hotel. Every night after my wife and children were asleep, I would log onto CompuServe to check my messages and check on the reps. I certainly did not mind the intrusion WPCorp made on my private life. The work was always exciting and interesting.

One of my best friends at WPCorp was Clive Winn. Back when I was in the drapery business, we were next-door neighbors. Clive worked as an undercover narcotics agent for the state of Utah and then as the director of the state police academy. About two years after I went to work for SSI, Clive went to work for the FBI, and he and his family moved away. When Clive's mother-in-law was diagnosed with cancer, his wife, Kathy, wanted to be near her. The FBI wouldn't move Clive to Southern California, so I helped him get a job as a WordPerfect rep in that area. A year later, Clive and his family moved back to Utah, so he could work at the company headquarters with our government accounts. He did a great job once he learned that to be a businessman he needed to continue thinking like a policeman rather than trying to be the nice guy. He was so good at what he did that in spite of some objections of cronyism, he was made vice president of sales in the summer of 1990.

Bruce asked Clive and me to come to his annual summer meeting of the general managers of all the international offices affiliated with WPCorp. The meeting was held in Nice, France, and was scheduled to begin on a Wednesday. Clive and I, along with four or five other people from the home office, left on Monday, so we could arrive a day early and rest before the meetings. On the first leg of our journey we were diverted from New York City to Philadelphia because of storms over JFK Airport. Knowing that we would likely miss every connection to Europe if we waited around, Clive and I grabbed our luggage and took a taxi to JFK, hoping to catch a late flight across the Atlantic. The others traveling with us stayed with the plane in Philadelphia, hoping the weather would clear.

Of course, while all the flights *into* JFK were delayed, the outbound flights all left on time. By the time we arrived, the last transatlantic flight had departed, and we were stuck in New York. We were determined not to arrive late for Bruce's meeting, however. We stayed in a hotel close to the airport and listened to gun shots through the night—which made ex-policeman Clive feel right at home—and in the morning we hopped on the Concorde to London. We arrived in the early evening and found a flight at 8:30 P.M. to Turin, Italy. After arriving in Italy, we rented a car and drove for four hours through the darkness to Nice. We would have made it a little sooner, had we been able to understand the tollroad system. Once I stopped trying to speak Spanish to the Italian toll-booth agents and Clive started talking with a $20 bill, we made good progress.

We arrived in Nice at 3:00 A.M. and got five hours sleep before the meetings started at 9:00 A.M. Bruce was amazed to see us and congratulated us on our ingenuity. It added to our sense of accomplishment when the others dragged in at 11:30 A.M., without their luggage and wearing the same clothes they had worn for three days.

We had fun explaining our marketing programs to the European general managers during the day and sitting under the stars on the beach figuring out how to improve them at night. One improvement we dreamed up applied to schools. We wanted very much to eliminate all the separate packages we had to manufacture for education, and we devised a clever way to do just that, while still giving schools a better price. We would allow schools to use seven free copies of our software for every copy they purchased. This was especially helpful in Europe, where they had trouble finding room for all the different SKUs (stock keeping units).

Much of the work I did for WordPerfect Corporation resembled this trip to Europe. I worked long hours, but the work was interesting and fun, and the settings were beautiful. My life was a series of great adventures.

One of the toughest decisions the board had to make in 1990 was whether or not to ship a 5.2 version of Word-Perfect for DOS. The DOS programmers weren't content sitting around, and they weren't overly anxious to help with the Windows product. By midsummer they were well into their next DOS version of WP. The Windows group was committed to using 5.1 as the basis for its version and was having a sufficiently tough time matching the 5.1 feature set without having to add the new 5.2 features as well. If we let the DOS group continue at full speed, it was very likely that the DOS version would come out right on the heels of the Windows version with an incompatible file format. For better or worse, Alan, Bruce, and I killed the 5.2 release, making our DOS customers wait for features that could have been available sooner. We felt the file incompatibilities 5.2 would create would severely hurt our chances in the Windows market.

WordPerfect Office was turning into a big problem. The program was useful, but it had a few weaknesses. The directory services, which listed everyone on the mail system along with their electronic addresses, could not hold more than one or two thousand entries. The scheduler, used to put together a meeting, was slow and sometimes unreliable. Installing the program was very difficult.

My approach to selling the product was to be very open about what it could and could not do. I wanted potential customers to understand the product's shortcomings, even if it meant lower sales. I thought we should discourage very large accounts from buying until a future release, when the program would be able to handle large numbers of users more effectively. Office had its strengths, and as long as we didn't oversell it, we would still find plenty of satisfied customers.

Not everyone liked my approach, however. The lead programmer on the project, who was also a vice president of development, started jumping on airplanes to visit customers and sell the product his way. His basic pitch was that Office was in its fifth year of a ten-year development effort. He promised that improvements were just around the corner, making Office the right choice for companies of all sizes. I tried to get Alan to stop the programmer from overselling, but Alan was overselling it himself. Alan loved to visit customers and tell them about all his products. He loved to promote them without reservation, and my suggestion that we explain the negative along with the positive was not appreciated.

Office's sales increased, but a newer version of the product was delayed and many customers had trouble getting Office to do the job they wanted it to do. I suggested we tell them we were sorry and use our resources to get an off-the-shelf product released as quickly as possible. Alan disagreed. He wanted to hire technicians to visit the customers and help them get the program up and running.

To me, "off-the-shelf" meant that a product was sold from a dealer's shelf, without someone from WordPerfect participating in its installation. A product that wasn't off-the-shelf, for instance, was All-in-One from DEC. A VAX customer might pay $25,000 for DEC's office automation product and then pay another $25,000 for systems engineers from DEC to come in and write code that would make the software work. That was not how I thought our software should be sold. We shouldn't have to send out a systems engineer or integrator to make it functional. As Scott McNealy from Sun Microsystems said: "When you go buy an automobile, you don't want to deal with a systems integrator. You don't want to have to have someone deliver it to your house, put you through a training program, reconstruct your garage and configure the automobile for you. You want to buy the automobile and drive it away."

Off-the-shelf software was the only type I thought we should be writing and selling. I certainly didn't mind if a dealer were to help a customer get going, but I didn't want us getting so involved that we were sending out a corps of technicians to help our customers work through the problems. I was afraid we would have to take responsibility for our customers' computer systems, and that responsibility was a lot more than we were prepared to handle. It also wasn't likely to bring us much money. If we actually had to touch a customer's machine for our product to work, then I believed we needed to reengineer the product.

This was probably the biggest disagreement Alan

and I had over the years and probably contributed to my leaving the company. Alan loved his products and his programmers, and he didn't seem to like me pointing out their deficiencies. He eventually sent out the technicians without my knowledge and behind my back, because he knew how strongly I was opposed to the idea.

Nonetheless, we put on our best face for COMDEX, despite our lack of a Windows word processor and the problems and delays with Office. André and our actor friends from Chicago did a show that was a take-off on the Broadway musical *City of Angels*. The star of the show was a detective who used different WordPerfect products to solve cases. The show had a lot of music, dancing, and acting, which helped us avoid getting too specific about our release dates. Our dealers and customers once again jammed into our booth to watch the show and pick up their freebies—this time detective hats.

By our Christmas party, the mood in the company was a little somber. We were starting to get some bad press, something that rarely happened before. The Gulf War was raging, and we were in the middle of a recession. We had cause to be cautious, but for some reason, I felt that we shouldn't be. When I spoke at the party, I asked everyone to close their eyes for a moment and ask themselves if it was time for caution because of the war and the recession, or if it was time to do more. I gave people time to listen to their feelings quietly and then asked for a show of hands. How many thought it was a time for caution? Only five or six hands went up. How many thought it was time to do more? Two thousand hands went up. Perhaps it was the way I asked the question, but I felt something inside. This was not a time to worry about the future. This was a time to promote our products more aggressively, to continue our building projects, and to plan optimistically for the future.

Our 1990 sales were at a hard-to-believe $452 million, and our pretax profits were up to 35 percent. The next year was going to be even better.

# 13

# Mid-Life Crisis

———

Bruce came up with our theme for 1991; it was our year to "think." Looking back, I have trouble understanding why we took our themes so seriously, but we did. The theme "think" came from experiences Bruce had had working on his family farm in Idaho. More than once, when Bruce had made a mistake, his father had gotten very frustrated and repeated the words "Think, think, think" with great intensity.

I liked the new theme because it uncovered another of our marketing problems. We were fairly good at making presentations and fairly good at giving customers a little time to talk, but many of our salespeople weren't processing the customers' information. To some, listening was only a pause in the presentation that gave customers a chance to feel important. Our salespeople needed to adapt what they were teaching to what our customers wanted to learn.

The theme was appropriate considering all the thinking we had to do to solve our problems, the biggest of which was the continued delay in the shipment of WordPerfect for Windows. Just one week after fall COMDEX in 1990, the Windows programmers informed us that the dates we had just given out in Las Vegas— a beta test to start in December and a product release at the end of February—would be impossible to meet. The most optimistic in the group felt the end of the second-quarter of 1991 was the earliest possible release date. The pessimists were saying August or September. We were in deep trouble.

The situation reminded me of the delays Lotus had gone through with a recent update of 1-2-3. First they announced a six-month delay. When the six months were up, they announced another six-month delay. I was worried we might suffer the same embarrassment. The right thing to do would be to tell our customers imme-diately that we knew our release date was in trouble, but I wanted to wait. We still didn't really know when the product would be ready, so I convinced myself we could hold off announcing the delay until we had better information.

Finally, in early February, we broke the news that our release date had slipped, but I was not entirely hon-est in the announcement. Rather than go with a realistic date or a vague date or no date at all, I announced a hoped-for second-quarter release, which was the most optimistic date from our most optimistic developer. My only excuse for announcing the earliest possible yet highly improbable date was that I was going through some sort of temporary insanity caused by a bad case of denial. I was afraid to face the difficulties that a longer delay might cause.

Few industry analysts or members of the press be-lieved we could make the second-quarter date, and word of our troubles was leaking out of the company. Amy Wohl, one of the more influential consultants, was quoted as saying we would make the second quarter re-lease date if there happened to be seventy-five days in

June. And she underestimated the time we would need by about sixty days.

We on the board had no one to blame for the delays but ourselves. The project directors we had chosen were inexperienced managers, and they made the mistakes inexperienced managers make. They were apt to make overly optimistic forecasts and had trouble chewing people out when they missed their deadlines. We waited too long to add more programmers to the project, always believing ourselves to be so close to a release that we didn't have time to train them and get any significant help from them. We also took too long to make our experienced DOS programmers get involved. They could have helped a little more, but we had difficulty convincing them that the Windows project was more important than anything else. Sales were still rising, and many thought things were going too well to be concerned.

It wasn't only the WordPerfect for Windows project that was behind schedule. As Alan and I met with each of the development groups to check on their progress, their stories were all the same. They all were behind schedule, and they all wanted more programmers. The DrawPerfect programmers, for example, were nowhere near a new release. Though their original product was well received in 1990, their program was already showing its age and starting to get less favorable reviews. Their next version, renamed WordPerfect Presentations, would not be ready for two more years.

The FormsPerfect developers were working on a project that would later be renamed InForms, and they were also making little progress. Their program was intended to help companies replace their printed forms with electronic forms. For example, if a company had a form for requesting reimbursement for medical expenses, InForms would allow employees to fill out the form on their computer screens and then route it automatically to the proper department. Bruce happened to call from Europe while Alan and I were meeting with the Forms group. He asked us to make sure the forms would be compatible with WordPerfect. We relayed his concern to the group, and they all looked sick. Somewhere along the way someone had decided that WordPerfect compatibility was not a high priority, and the product (which would not come out until mid-1993) couldn't create forms that could be used with WordPerfect.

WordPerfect Office was now six years into an eleven-year development, and a release that would deliver on all our promises was still a long way off. One big problem was getting all the different Office development groups to work together. By now we had teams for PC networks, for the Macintosh, and for UNIX, DG, and DEC machines, and none of the groups seemed to be willing to work out their differences. They couldn't decide on the maximum number of enclosures that could be attached to a message. The VAX group wanted an unlimited number of attachments; the Mac programmers felt 100 files was more than enough; and the PC group allowed only 30 files to accompany a message. Of course, if someone using a VAX were to send 101 attachments with a message, the Mac and PC Office versions would crash, but that was not incentive enough to get the groups to agree on a standard. The VAX group felt they had to have an unlimited number, because their VAX competitors offered an unlimited number. The Mac programmers were certain 30 was too few, but the PC group was already shipping a product with a limitation of 30 files, and they weren't about to change it.

Unfortunately, Alan didn't have much time to work with the different development groups. He was busy giving speeches, collecting awards, and attending industry conferences. Even if he had been around the office, we had so many projects going that he couldn't have given all of them much attention. In his absence, his development leaders had to do a lot more on their own and sometimes got off track. To try to help get things back under control, Freida, his assistant, and I conspired to limit the number of awards that Alan could accept to two per month. I wondered if all the attention we were receiving had anything to do with *Forbes* having identified Alan and Bruce as among the four hundred richest individuals in the United States.

Although my thoughts didn't carry a lot of weight with the programmers, I did try to figure out what needed to be done to get things under control. For years we had tried to produce a successful family of products, and the result was more software projects than we could handle. As I decided which products to continue and which products to cut, I realized that our product successes seemed to be those that were most closely related to word processing. WordPerfect Office distributed messages or documents, and DrawPerfect created figures and charts for documents. Perhaps as a result of the document connection, both products sold fairly well. DataPerfect and PlanPerfect were applications that had little to do with documents, and neither had sold very well. I decided that the focus of our development should be on word processing and on those products that were closely associated with word processing, and I never hesitated to promote my new theory.

At the end of February, IBM asked me to come to Boca Raton for a secret meeting. This was yet another instance of someone pulling our chain. The appointment was for 8:00 A.M., which was 6:00 A.M. Utah time, so I was in a bad mood when the meeting began. It was almost more than I could bear when I found out that I was there for two days of intensive OS/2 training. There were five or six of us present, representing all the largest software companies except Microsoft, and we were to be IBM's audience for a dress rehearsal of their OS/2 seminar. I listened respectfully for as long as I could, which was about thirty minutes, and then raised my hand. The presenter asked me to hold my question until the end of the presentation, but I told him I would leave if I could not interrupt. He reluctantly agreed to let me speak, and I announced that I would rather be at an Amway recruiting dinner than listen to two days of technical presentations. I wanted to know why we were wasting our time talking about OS/2 when Microsoft had clearly won the war of the GUI operating systems.

What I really wanted to know was why IBM was trying to copy Microsoft with a technical approach to marketing. I remembered that IBM had introduced their new Personal Computer AT model with a huge party in Dallas called "Partners in Pride." They had invited almost everyone in the industry to a beautiful hotel to give us great food and entertainment and to introduce their new product with a few short presentations. That was the IBM I understood. Now, however, they were playing the part of the nerd, trying to be like Microsoft by offering boring classes on graphics capabilities and memory management. This was not the IBM I used to know.

IBM tried to keep me happy by cutting down on the amount of technical information included in the meetings, but most of what they presented went over my head. The one thing I did understand was that IBM was not ready to give up on OS/2. If they had to turn into nerds to win the operating system business, they were willing to give it a try. They were willing to do almost anything to win back control of the market, even giving away their operating system for a while and paying Microsoft to include a copy of Windows with OS/2. That way, computer users could run DOS, Windows, and OS/2 programs by buying only OS/2.

As I sat through the meetings, I wanted to believe that IBM had a chance. Our long-term success was, I thought, dependent on diversity. If the world was filled only with Windows machines, then Microsoft would have a tremendous advantage. If instead the world was filled with DOS, Windows, OS/2, Macintosh, and UNIX machines, we could maintain our advantage in the personal computer word-processing market.

My advice to IBM was to not play the role of the nerd.

I hoped they would hang on to their old polished and professional image, and not walk around with un-combed hair and calculators on their belts. I felt their seminar would have been much better if their presentations were more exciting, and if they had taken the participants down to the beach to eat a great dinner and listen to a Beach Boys concert, which would have been more in character.

Microsoft was very good at making it tough for IBM to push OS/2. They were promising to deliver tools to port Windows applications to OS/2 and encouraging developers interested in OS/2 to write Windows versions first. Later, long after most companies had decided to go with a "Windows first" strategy, Microsoft decided not to deliver the OS/2 porting tools. Worse still, once IBM told the world that OS/2 would run DOS programs better than DOS, and Windows programs better than Windows, Microsoft reminded the world that IBM's right to distribute the Windows portion of OS/2 would expire in a few years, leading some people to conclude that OS/2 would eventually be a dead end. I had little hope that IBM would be able to win out over Microsoft, but I admired their tenacity.

By May of 1991, we still were not showing much progress with a WPwin release. We were a little closer to getting into a beta test, but nowhere close to releasing a product. I dreaded making the announcement of another delay. While I was thinking about how to break the news, I came up with an idea for an ad campaign. I was tired of having everyone focus on our release date, so I proposed to our ad agency that we have a contest for our customers to guess how many copies of WPwin we would ship in the first month the product was released. I hoped to shift the focus from our weakness, which was our tardiness, to our strength, which was the great demand that existed for the product.

The first ad in my proposed campaign would an-nounce the contest, giving the customers details about expected demand for the product and our capacity to manufacture it. We would explain that the purpose of the contest was to get as many people as possible to help us come up with an accurate sales forecast. The second ad would announce various statistics about the guesses we received. We would publish the highest estimate, the lowest, and the average for all estimates. We would also let people know how the product was progressing. A third ad would announce our preparations for the shipment of the product, a fourth the product release, and a fifth the winner of the contest. Hopefully, in the sixth and last ad of the campaign, we could announce to the world that we had the best-selling word processor for Windows.

At first our ad agency had trouble with the idea. Of course, since I was the executive vice president, they told me they liked it, but when they showed us a possible layout for the first ad, they had changed the contest into a sweepstakes. The customers only had to send in an entry (not a sales estimate), with the lucky winners chosen from a random drawing. It took a lot of persuading and a little emotion to get them to understand that it had to be a contest. I wanted customers to think about the huge number of packages we were going to ship, and I was frankly very curious as to what they had to say. In the end I got my way, and we went ahead with the campaign.

Getting the agency to agree to my idea reminded me that while ad firms can be a great help, they sometimes overestimate their competence and underestimate the taste of some of their clients. When asking them for ideas, I sometimes felt like they were using a trick I had learned in my drapery days. When parents decided to let children choose their own drapes, I found the children almost always chose colors that were too bright. To prevent them from choosing something I knew their mothers would hate, I would give them only three choices, making sure that two of the choices were so bad that they would take the one I wanted them to take. When an ad agency gave a presentation, I felt like I would see only one option that was reasonable and a few others that were obviously horrible. More than once I wished they would have treated me like a thinking adult, rather than like an incompetent executive who was not to be taken seriously.

Our first ad in the WPwin series had a picture of Clive Winn asking customers to call an 800 number to help him forecast the first month's sales of WPwin. He offered $25,000 cash to the person with the estimate closest to actual sales.

We held auditions for operators from our information services group and selected those who were friendliest to take the calls that came in from the ad. We trained them not only to ask for names, addresses, phone numbers, and estimates, but also to express appreciation to the callers for their help and to engage them in a conversation about their plans for Windows and our Windows product.

From the thousands of people who called, we selected a few and sent a photographer out to take pictures of them, which we included in the second ad. In addition to the high, low, and average of all estimates, we included explanations of some of the different ways people had arrived at their forecasts. Some of the calculations were very complicated.

One of the callers was a Microsoft employee. He happened to guess that our sales would be many times greater than the current sales of Microsoft Word for Windows, so we put his estimate in the second ad along with a map of Washington State. Microsoft called in a huff to complain about the low blow, and that made the whole campaign a lot more fun. Instead of wringing our hands, worrying about how late we were, we thought about how many copies of the product we would sell and how much Microsoft hated all the hype.

It was very gratifying to me to read Stewart Alsop's

comments about the ad campaign. Mr. Alsop published a popular industry newsletter and later became editor-in-chief for *InfoWorld*. He wrote: "This is one of those incredibly creative marketing ideas that can only be done once. . . . By asking customers to predict the success of the product, WordPerfect manages to get the customers involved in trying to make the thing successful." In a different article, written for a trade publication in England, he called the first ad "one of the most creative advertisements ever seen in the PC industry." That was a nice reward considering the struggle it had been to get our agency to support the campaign.

I had a very strange experience in July. My dad, who by now had retired from Harris Corporation and had come to work in our sales department in Utah, called to ask me for an appointment. This was unusual, considering that his house was right next door to mine and we saw each other almost every day. When we met he looked very sad and explained that Bruce had asked him to meet with me. Bruce wanted him to tell me that I would have to change, because I was too hard on people and too many people were afraid of me.

I had trouble understanding why my dad had been asked to convey the message, so I called Bruce and requested a meeting. By the time I reached Bruce's house, Alan was there as well. They explained their concerns, and I told them I didn't know how to do my job any other way. I asked them if I was any more difficult or any harder to work with than I had been during the last five or ten years. I had my share of enemies and some people were afraid of me, but this was nothing new. I asked them to play me or trade me and told them I couldn't do my job without upsetting a few people.

I left Bruce's house thinking things were settled. I was not very impressed that they had put my father in the middle of the discussion, but I knew they were under a lot of stress because of the Windows delays. Bruce was getting pressure from his international offices to release a Windows product, and Microsoft was beginning to cut into our market shares in Europe.

Alan was in a difficult situation as well. Many of the development project dates were slipping, and like me, he was having to disappoint a few people. He was very determined to get a WordPerfect 6.0 project started right away. The programmers doing the 5.1 Windows version also wanted responsibility for WPwin 6.0, but they wouln't be able to work on a new project for another few months. Alan felt he had no choice but to disappoint the 5.1 Windows programmers and give the 6.0 Windows project to another group.

There was more to what Bruce was trying to tell me than I knew at the time. The vice president of development in charge of WordPerfect Office was convinced I needed to change, and he had been lobbying with Alan, Bruce, and others to have another person elected to the board of directors to dilute my influence. He was sure that Bruce and Alan went along with my views too much of the time, and that I was leading the company to ruin.

Even if the vice president hadn't been lobbying against me, I wouldn't have been too happy with him. Office was not moving forward very quickly, and instead of resolving the problems, this well-intentioned leader was giving lectures about seven habits of effective leaders from a book by Stephen Covey. He made his teams take time away from their programming efforts to attend lectures and do homework based on the ideas in the book. The VP also advocated using conflict as a way to get things done. I wondered how conflict could be the answer when it seemed that what the Office group needed was some conflict resolution. Unless a way could be found to get those groups back on track, we would soon be seven years into a twelve-year project.

I asked Alan why this vice president was allowed to teach whatever he wanted. As I had explained in my management training, I expected the board to define the correct company principles—not any and every vice president. Alan told me not to worry. He had given the go-ahead for the lectures, and he would take care of the problem. I found the conversation very disappointing, because I realized then that Alan was not involved in what I had been trying to teach. He just wanted everyone to be happy.

I did learn a lot from this incident, however. For years we had used "We teach correct principles and let employees govern themselves" as the basis for our management philosophy. Although we hadn't always done a good job implementing the philosophy, I felt we had at least understood it. Now, I realized we didn't.

If we were actually to adopt the philosophy, we would have to complete at least four steps. First we had to define the correct principles for WordPerfect Corporation. Then we had to teach them. Next we had to trust the employees to govern themselves. Finally, the employees had to be accountable for governing their actions with the correct principles.

If any of the four steps was missing, the management system wouldn't work. If the principles weren't defined, then any teaching was likely to be in error. If the principles were defined but not taught, the employees would be in the dark. If the employees were supervised so completely that they had no freedom, then there was no opportunity for the learning and individual initiative that come with self-government. If the employees refused to be accountable to the principles when governing their actions, then the first three steps were useless. Although we had done a fairly good job of fulfilling step three— turning people loose over the years—we always had trouble with steps one, two, and four. Even all the work I had done with my management training courses was not very effective. Without the full support of Alan and Bruce, I couldn't be certain that my principles were correct for the company.

The fundamental problem I had with Bruce and Alan and others in the company who were defining their own principles was the difference in our definitions of the word *correct*. I thought *correct* meant "as defined by the board," but many others in the company thought it meant "principles that are recognized as true or good." To me, a certain principle's truth or validity according to a certain writer, a certain authority, or a certain business school was totally irrelevant. What should have mattered most was how the owners of the company wanted to conduct their business. Only the owners had the authority to define right and wrong within the company.

A day or so later I had a chance to explain to Alan and the vice president why I thought it wasn't possible for everyone in the company to define the correct principles, but the vice president wasn't convinced. He felt he should be given enough responsibility and authority to define and adapt principles for his own group. He felt the title of vice president carried with it certain rights and privileges, because that was the way the job was defined in the normal business world. Of course, I felt that the duties of a vice president should be defined by the employer, not by the rest of the world. There were no published rules of business that required the owners to meet a particular set of expectations.

In spite of Alan's feeling that our disagreement was not a big problem, employees started telling me about a petition that was being circulated. Claims were being made that I was ruining careers without good reason and manipulating the board to my own advantage. I was more hurt than angry with the rumors. This vice president and a few people around him were assuming that if someone's advancement was impeded by my actions, it was because of my personal feelings for that person. That a particular employee may have messed up badly or that there may have been an equally valid reason for lack of advancement didn't occur to them. My guilt was presumed, without a full view of the evidence.

Later, in a design review meeting with this vice president and a few programmers from the Macintosh Office group, Alan finally realized the problem was more than a simple disagreement. The programmers explained what they were doing and what their priorities were, and I asked why their 4.0 version had a higher priority than their 3.1 version. Since 3.1 was still unreleased, I wanted to know why a future version would get more attention. The vice president, who had been fairly quiet to this point, lost his temper, raised his voice, and answered so angrily that he bared his teeth and spit as he spoke. The intensity of his emotion convinced Alan that this was not a problem that would go away quickly. My question did not deserve such an emotional response. Alan soon put someone else in charge of WordPerfect Office and moved the vice president to another position in the company.

I didn't enjoy my job too much after this. For close to ten years, I had been the person most responsible for running the company. It came as somewhat of a shock to learn that a lot of what I did wasn't wanted or appreciated. Bruce and Alan were quick to admit that many of the things I did were brilliant, but I could now see that we had numerous disagreements over the running of the company. They were now beginning to wonder if I wasn't more of a bother than I was worth.

In the fall, we started to talk seriously about going public. I had asked Bruce and Alan for help with a potential estate tax problem, and this led to a discussion of their estate tax problems. Their situation was much more complicated than mine, because their net worth was so much more than mine. If both parents in one of the families were to die, the only way to pay the estate taxes without risking the financial security of their children would be to sell off enough stock to pay the taxes within six months of the deaths. Selling what could amount to $500 million worth of stock within a six-month period wasn't something they could count on, however. As we talked, we came to the conclusion that the best answer would either be to go public or to put ourselves in a position where we could go public at any time. Duff Thompson, our general counsel, and I were asked to start looking into the possibility of a public stock offering.

The WPwin roll-out came off without a major problem. As soon as the product shipped in November, our ads showed trucks lining up to pick up the software and software packages arriving at dealer shelves. As we had hoped, sales were terrific, and for the month of November we outsold Word for Windows. Thirty days after the release, Price Waterhouse sifted through all our invoices and all the estimates and came up with the winner of our contest. The $25,000 was won by a single mom from the Midwest who had just adopted a baby. We couldn't have asked for a better ending to our ad campaign script.

Our success was not cause for a huge celebration, however. Microsoft had introduced a new version of WindWord at COMDEX (their official abbreviation for Word for Windows was WinWord, but I liked to add the extra d), and the new version included some new features ours didn't have. Among other things, they included a grammar checker and a feature called Word Art. I liked to think the features weren't very useful, but they did look very nice in a demonstration.

Soon after COMDEX, Bruce sent Alan and me a memo. He asked if the three of us should still be the only ones to run the company. He thought it might be time to delegate more responsibility and rely on the opinions of some other people in the company, rather than only on our own feelings and judgment. He wrote that he was a little embarrassed by our image, which seemed to him to be unprofessional at times. He also felt it was time to go public.

I thought the memo was a little odd and assumed he was venting his frustration over Microsoft's new features. I told him that I thought we knew what we were doing and that I was still able and willing to do my job.

I also asked him if he still wanted to do his part. I heard later that he interpreted my question as an insult and decided then that one of us had to go. I had not intended to question his competence. I asked the question because I wondered if he was trying to tell us that he was ready to slow down. I had no idea that he was trying to tell me to take a less active role in running the company.

I did agree with Bruce's desire to go public, but it was not because it might improve our image or solve the estate tax issues. For years our international offices had operated with a lot of independence. I was hoping the initial public offering (IPO) preparations would force us to rein in the international branches. At the very least, I hoped we would get better reports back from the offices, so we could get our tax returns finished before the last minute of the last filing extension.

On the surface, 1991 looked like a great year. We had sales of $533 million and our normally high profit percentage. We were so sure that our record-breaking sales levels would continue that we gave large bonuses to all of our 2,894 employees. Personally, however, the year was not a great one. I was worn out, not only because of our ongoing conflict with Microsoft, but from all the infighting and the politics. I finally thought I knew how to run the company, and I realized that not too many people cared.

I did have one satisfying moment at the end of the year. Duff Thompson reminded me that when we recruited him in 1987, I had told him we would have sales of half a billion dollars within five years. Although he had trouble believing me at the time, he noted in December that we had made it with a year to spare.

# 14

# MAJOR SURGERY

Our theme for 1992 was "focus." This would prove to be an ironic choice, because at the start of the year we were falling apart, and by midear the company would become "unleashed," extending itself in many different directions.

After finishing 1991 with very high sales, we expected sales to continue upward, the same way they had with every other new WordPerfect release. To our dismay, however, January sales were very low, and February sales were only slightly better. This was a problem the company had not faced before.

We were also disappointed by the lukewarm WPwin reviews, which complained that the product was a little slow and a little buggy; they were right. Long gone were the days when I could take a WordPerfect review home and be certain I would enjoy reading it.

We needed to get a cleaner and faster version of WPwin out the door, but it would take some time.

Microsoft was heavily promoting DDE (dynamic data exchange), which was a set of specifications they defined that allowed different Windows programs to exchange information. In theory, if we wrote our program to support Microsoft's specifications, a WPwin document could give information to and receive information from other programs. Our programmers wanted to delay the release so the new feature could be included in the product.

A low point for the company occurred in late January at Demo '92, an annual industry conference hosted by Stewart Alsop where software companies showed off their new products. Devin Durrant, our marketing director for WordPerfect for Windows, had been invited to participate in a product shoot-out with Microsoft Word for Windows and Ami Pro from Lotus. At my suggestion, Devin stressed our file compatibility across different computer platforms. The other demonstrators showed off their flashiest features. Alan, Clive, Duff, and I were all there to see Devin get ripped apart by the other presenters as well as by the audience.

On our way home from Palm Springs, where the conference was held, our plane was prevented from landing in Salt Lake City because of fog, and we were forced to fly all the way back to Ontario, California. Duff, Clive, and I rented a car and drove home rather than waiting for the fog to lift. The eleven-hour ride through the darkness was over in what seemed like a couple of hours. After getting beaten so badly in the shoot-out, we needed to figure out how we were going to hold things together. We had three thousand employees and ten million customers around the world, and we felt like they were counting on us to come up with the right decisions and strategies. It is difficult to put into words the excitement we felt trying to find solutions to seemingly impossible problems. We were in a battle to the death with Microsoft, and we were hurt, but we were three friends who, together, could accomplish almost anything.

By February we had figured out why our sales were so slow, and our future didn't look as bleak. Our unusually high October 1991 sales were the result of our distributors ordering too much of our DOS product, thinking we would have trouble shipping it once the Windows version was ready. Our unusually high November sales were due to our distributors ordering too much WordPerfect for Windows, afraid we would have to ration the product as we had with WordPerfect 5.0 and 5.1 for DOS. As it turned out, we had no trouble delivering product, and our distributors were left with larger inventories than they needed. Although our sell-through (the actual sales made to customers) was good considering the lukewarm reviews, it was not nearly good enough to drain off the surplus immediately.

Once we realized why our sales were higher than they should have been in October and November of 1991, it was fairly easy to predict that sales would improve quickly. At the rate distributor inventories were shrinking, we could expect our sales to return to normal levels by the end of March or early April 1992. It was unfortunate for our IPO plans that the first quarter was so disappointing, but we had no reason to panic.

Early in the year, we met with our accountants from Price Waterhouse to learn what we needed to do to prepare for the IPO. They suggested changes to our management team, changes to our accounting and reporting methods, changes to our salaries and benefits, and more. Although we weren't ready to adopt all their suggestions, we could see the need to reorganize. Our business was split into about fourteen different corporations and one partnership. We wanted to consolidate most of the branches of the business into one corporation before going ahead with the IPO.

We took SoftCopy, a manufacturing corporation owned by the three of us on the board, and split it into two parts. The part that produced our software was merged into WordPerfect Corporation. The other part, which did work for many of our competitors, survived as a smaller company at a new location. One effect of the change was to increase our American employee count by five hundred, raising it up to almost thirty-three hundred. Another effect was to increase my stock in WPCorp from 0.2 percent to 1 percent in exchange for the 20 percent share I had owned in the manufacturing company.

In February, Bruce sent Alan and me another memo. Bruce had gone to a software store in the local mall and had left upset, because the shelf space devoted to our products was much less than the space reserved for Microsoft and Lotus. He asked if our marketing was as good as we thought it was. He asked again if the three of us were capable of leading the company. In my reply, I told him plainly that I was good at what I did and mentioned that some of our problems might have more to do with our products than our marketing.

In March, Duff, Clive, and I went to a Software Publishers' Association conference in Seattle. We spent more time discussing a new sales program for large accounts than we did attending the meetings. Duff was convinced we needed to have an option in the program to sell directly to large customers. Selling direct was something I wanted very much to avoid. From 1980 until 1988, we had sold direct to large corporations, to governments, and to schools. The result was a lot of unhappy dealers, who were convinced we were stealing their business, and a bunch of slow-paying customers. I believed it was more important to keep our thousands of dealers happy and motivated to sell our products than it was for us to try to sell direct to a few accounts. With only about 250 reps in the United States and Canada, I didn't see how we could handle enough accounts to make a direct-sales program worth the bad feelings it was bound to create.

Duff was adamant that we needed to establish direct relationships with our customers. He felt so strongly about it that he had actually written down his arguments on paper, in what sounded a lot like a legal brief. He was sure we were missing opportunities and offending some customers with our unwillingness to establish a closer relationship.

We were close to Egghead's headquarters, so when I saw how difficult it would be to change his mind, I rented a car and took him out to talk to one of our real dealers. Egghead's president and two of their vice presidents gave us a couple of hours, and Duff explained what he wanted to do. They listened politely to his arguments and then explained what they were doing to sell our products. Duff, though impressed by what they said, would not change his mind. Some customers were telling us they wanted to buy directly from us, and Duff didn't want to turn them down.

If I would have been a little smarter, I might have realized that Duff must have been talking to Alan. Alan and I had disagreed earlier about how much technical support we should offer the customer, and I suspect he also disagreed with my insistence that we not sell directly to large accounts. I can think of no other explanation for Duff's maintaining his position when I was against it so much.

While it would have been easier to give the customers what they wanted, I couldn't believe that "the customer is always right." In fact, I had come to the conclusion that the person who coined the phrase had actually meant to say "the customer always gripes," for I had seen many occasions when the customer was definitely wrong. Some customers did not want to pay a fair price. Some asked for more than their fair share of service and support. Some even lied to us to try to get back part or all of their money.

In this case, Duff and Alan were listening to customers who said they needed to buy product directly from us in order to develop a closer and better relationship. For years I had listened to the same plea, and in almost every case the customer was interested in establishing a direct relationship only so they could attempt to negotiate a better price and ask for additional services. I frankly wanted to use our dealers as protection from these negotiations and to insulate us from the individual pleas for pricing relief. I knew we were too eager to please when a client asked us for something.

For example, I had recently visited a large financial company in New York City. They threatened to use another word processor unless we were willing to provide them with a part-time network specialist. They were going through some support budget cuts, and they expected us to make up for their losses. I did my best to explain our off-the-shelf way of doing business, but they were not impressed. They wanted help and they wanted it immediately. The quality of our product didn't matter if we weren't willing to give in to their demands.

This was not an unusual circumstance. As large corporations made the transition from the full-service old world to the self-service new world, they were desperately trying to find a way to extract the same level of service from their vendors, even though they were paying much lower prices. They acted like spoiled rich people who were trying to save money on their vacation by going to a two-star resort instead of the five-star resort they were used to. I imagined them sitting in their boats in the middle of a lake, yelling at the top of their lungs, "Where is my drink, where is my lunch, where is my magazine, and who is going to row my boat?" I imagined myself as the manager of the resort, politely yelling back to them to row their boats to the shore so I could explain where they needed to go to get what they wanted. Of course, they were not likely to pick up their oars, but I certainly wasn't going to swim out and row for them. It would be foolish to give in to their demands and offer them five-star service at a two-star price.

I don't mean to imply that customers should be ignored or treated shabbily. I sincerely believe in being cordial, fair, and honest with them. Their requests,

comments, concerns, and needs should always be carefully considered and used as a valuable source of information. Their demands should, however, be kept in
perspective. Sometimes they may not know what they
want, sometimes they may change their minds, and
sometimes they are not willing to pay for all that they
want.

Though I say customers are not always right, I do
believe they deserve good value for their money and the
best service possible within the limits of what is profitable. When a customer asks for more than this, however,
I don't think it's right to give in. It's not fair to other
customers to offer a higher level of service to those companies that complain the most.

The Monday after we returned from Seattle was
Monday, March 23, 1992—the day Bruce and Alan told
me about their plan to expand the board and change my
duties. We spent close to three hours in that meeting,
much of the time discussing our differences. I felt as if
the company were in a boxing match with Microsoft,
who, in hitting us with their Windows strategy, had delivered a very hard blow. I thought we had been stag-
gered by the punch. We needed to cover up and conserve
our strength, so we would have the resources to come out
fighting in the next round with WordPerfect 6.0. Bruce
and Alan agreed that we were in trouble, but disagreed
with my conservative strategy. They wanted to retaliate
immediately, thinking we already had good products
and that what we needed was to counterpunch with a
more aggressive and expensive approach to marketing.

They were ready to consider acquisitions, bundles,
and strategic alliances, but I wanted to keep things simple. They were ready to hire technical reps to go to customer sites to help them install and use our products, but
I wanted to keep our hands off our customers' networks,
for fear we would become entangled in their support
problems. They were ready to sell directly to customers,
but I wanted to use our dealers. Bruce wanted a new

image, but I was happy with the one we had. After all the struggles that resulted from preannouncing our Windows product, I wanted to avoid the practice forever, but they wanted to tell the world what was coming right away. I wanted to define and teach correct principles and maintain a flat organization, but they wanted to use a more democratic approach and bring in a few experienced people from outside the company.

As I talked with them, I never considered going along with what they wanted me to do. For right or wrong, I had confidence in my decisions and ideas. I couldn't have run the business for all those years without it. I cared too much for the company and held on to my opinions too strongly to accept a passive role in its future.

After the meeting, I went back to work as if nothing had happened. When Bruce and Alan did not talk to me the next day, I wasn't very concerned. I was still absorbed in my day-to-day work, and felt like nothing was going to happen. Duff came into my office near the end of the day on Tuesday to say he wasn't sure what they would do. He thought they were frozen in place, not wanting me to leave, but not wanting to back down. It was probably a mistake, but I told Duff I didn't think they had the courage to run the company without me.

Until Wednesday morning, when Bruce and Alan came into my office to tell me they were taking me up on my offer to leave for six months, I never for a moment considered they would let me go. I had always put their interests and the interests of the company ahead of my own, and I had always given them my best. As what they said sank in, all I wanted to do was get out of there without them seeing me shed any tears. I did manage to thank them both and wish them well before I left.

That afternoon my departure and the new members of the board of directors were announced to the directors and vice presidents in the company. As the news spread throughout the company, some people were reportedly dancing in the aisles, while others were calling me with their condolences. By the next afternoon, I could see that I wouldn't have to wait six months to find out if Alan and Bruce wanted me back to run their company. The organization had changed so much in one day that I knew they would never try to undo the changes.

The realization that almost all of my friends and many of my neighbors and relatives worked for the company caused me to reconsider my "sabbatical." I felt lonely and friendless. I didn't mind giving up the money, because I had enough, but giving up the daily association with my friends was an incredibly high price to pay to defend my business philosophy.

In a weak moment on Thursday afternoon, I went back to talk to Bruce and Alan and beg them for a job. The three of us met for an hour, and I told them I was willing to do anything they wanted me to do. They seemed relieved and happy to have me back on their terms. No announcement would have to be made to the press, and the three of us could still be friends. We decided it would be better if I didn't return to the office right away, so that the new board members could have some time to feel comfortable in their new positions. I had no problem with that. I was ready to take some time off.

My wife was relieved to hear I was going back. She had been afraid that my leaving the company might be hard on her relationship with her family. My oldest daughter, Wendy, was furious with me, however. She accused me of standing up for my principles only until I had to live with the consequences, and she was right.

The next morning I got a call at home from Spencer Katt, the rumor columnist for *PC Week*. He had heard I was leaving WordPerfect Corporation and wanted to hear my side of the story. I told him the rumor was false. My job description was changing, but I was staying with the company.

After I hung up, I got a call from Alan. He was sorry, but an announcement of my resignation had just been released to the press. Apparently, after I left the previous day, Bruce had called John Lewis, one of the new board members, with the news that I was staying. John got very red in the face at hearing the news and said something like, "You own the company, so I guess you don't have to consult your new board if you don't want to." The next morning, Bruce and Alan called a board meeting to discuss their decision to let me return. By the time the meeting ended, Duff had voiced his opinion that I wouldn't be happy coming back with a different role, and the new board had decided I should not return. Although I'm not sure Duff had my best interests in mind, he was right in what he said. I would have been miserable witnessing the transformation of the company up close.

Throughout the weekend our phone never stopped ringing. Whenever the press called, I told them that my departure was a mutual decision. I was repeating the same story the people at WPCorp were giving out to help make the transition as painless as possible. I still owned 1 percent of the company and hoped that it would continue to do well. My kids were not as good at controlling their comments, however. When the *Salt Lake Tribune* called to ask if ours was the home of the Pete Peterson who worked at WordPerfect, my daughter Ellen burst into tears and told them that I had been fired.

My youngest children, David and Julie, shed a few tears. All they understood was that their dad was out of work, and they assumed that meant we would soon be out of money. They were too little to understand that interest income was as good as a salary. My middle son, Joseph, seemed to take the news without much concern, but Sam and Wendy were very angry that I had been asked to go after working so hard for so many years.

The most inconvenient call came at 2:00 A.M. on Sunday morning. Someone from the Associated Press phoned to ask if I was the Pete Peterson who had resigned from WordPerfect Corporation. The reporter had been calling all the Petersons in the Provo/Orem phone book, trying to locate the right one. Since my real name is Willard, he must have awakened a lot of families before dialing our number. He asked whether I could give him an interview immediately, or whether I would be willing to make an appointment for later that morning. I asked for a 9:00 A.M. appointment and then spent the rest of the night wishing I had talked right then, so I could have gone back to sleep.

The next few months were difficult. I experienced all the typical emotions of those who lose their jobs. I went through the normal periods of denial, sadness, depression, anger, and resignation. It was hard for me to lose my WordPerfect identity, with its semi-celebrity status. I missed the lunches and the tennis matches in the late afternoon, when we worked through all our important problems. I missed battling with Microsoft. I found out that retiring at forty-three is not as attractive as most people imagine.

Soon after I left, Bruce and Alan met with all the employees to explain what was happening in the company. They made a big point of talking about the new WordPerfect, which was now a "WordPerfect unleashed," and hinted that I had been the person responsible for holding the company back. Now that I was gone, the company was free to become more aggressive and to experiment with more ideas.

In June, extravagant press conferences were held on both coasts to introduce the new, unleashed version of WordPerfect. Their new WISE (WordPerfect Information Systems Environment) product strategy was introduced, and almost all of the upcoming products were preannounced. Possible alliances were mentioned. Acquisitions were suggested.

The company reorganization took place throughout the summer. An executive committee was formed. A new management layer was created for senior vice presidents. A vice president was hired to supervise the manufacturing department. More attorneys were hired. A vice president was brought in from Europe to run the marketing department. A new director of MIS was hired. Dan Campbell was hired away from Price Waterhouse to be the chief financial officer and help with the IPO, and he brought a few more accountants with him. Over the next year, WPCorp would grow by more than eight-hundred employees, even though its sales would reportedly increase only slightly.

Not all of the changes that created this larger, unleashed version of WordPerfect Corporation had to do with the size and shape of the organization. More and longer meetings and longer workdays were the norm. Paperwork, which included detailed business plans from all marketing units and field reps, increased. Technical reps were hired to help large accounts with their problems. Large accounts were offered a direct purchase program. In a year, WPCorp would acquire three companies and announce an alliance with Borland, the self-proclaimed barbarians of the industry.

As all these changes were taking place, Bruce and Alan were paying me to be a consultant for the company. The consulting agreement, which was to run for two or three years, was not very satisfying for me. I made the mistake of thinking they wanted my advice, so I tried to give it to them. Whenever I sent them a report, however, they wondered how I continued to know so much about the company. Rather than act on my words of counsel, they looked for ways to plug their information leaks. They soon disconnected me from the company network and then from the company phone system. A few of my old friends were given lectures on confidentiality. It finally became clear to me that Bruce and Alan did not want my help. The consulting fee was hush money, and my only responsibilities were to keep quiet and not cause trouble.

In December, Dan Campbell dropped by my house to explain some of the accounting changes they were making to prepare for the IPO. As I listened, it became clear to me that my share of the company was going to be diluted, so I offered to sell out. Even if selling my stock before the IPO meant receiving less money, I was ready to end the relationship and get on with my life. I am sure Alan and Bruce felt the same way. On Christmas Eve, I signed the agreements that returned my stock to them and terminated all our business relationships.

# 15

# DECLINING YEARS OR A REBIRTH?

———

I may never know whether WordPerfect Corporation is better off without me. Their sales for 1992 did not increase much over those for 1991, but they did manage to weather the Windows storm without any major problems. By mid-1993 they claimed to have a 51 percent share of the Windows word-processing market, which was quite an accomplishment considering that they did it before releasing WPwin 6.0. Their alliances, technical reps, increased advertising, direct sales to large accounts, and preannouncements don't seem to have hurt them. They are now delivering on the promises made at their press conferences in 1992, and their new products look very impressive. Even their hiring of fourteen hundred additional employees in the year and a half after I left may not turn out to be a mistake if sales improve.

I also may never know the reasons that pushed them into letting me go. I suspect that our philosophical differences were probably less important than the personal issues. I probably offended Bruce more than I thought when I misinterpreted his memos. I thought he was asking to get out of the company; he was probably saying he wanted to take charge. For Alan's part, I think I made too many enemies inside the company over the years, and he finally got tired of defending me.

Of one thing, however, I feel certain. Falling on my sword was good for me personally. Near the end I was short-tempered and impatient much of the time. I felt unappreciated and was worn out from all the strain of holding on to customers while they waited for our Windows product. I needed to get away and find an identity apart from WordPerfect Corporation. I needed to remember how much my family meant to me, and I needed time to try to convince them that I loved them more than I loved my work.

Although I am no longer as emotionally involved in all that happens next door at WPCorp, I still get discouraged watching them go through their ongoing remodeling process. Some of the changes are minor, like requiring all employees to wear or carry their identification badges. Some changes, like the additional layers of management, or the extra hours the employees are expected to work, seem like major steps in the wrong direction. I have to admit, however, that Bruce and Alan accomplished much of what they set out to do. The image they now project to the world is a little more professional, a little less naive, a little more aggressive, and one which more closely resembles those of other companies.

A sales rep who would have been happy to live and die in Tennessee now has to consider moving away from friends and family to move up in the company. Instead of having three layers of management above him, he now has five or six. No longer is most of his time spent face-to-face with customers, shaking hands, grinning, and looking them in the eye. Now he is writing business plans, analyzing his customers' businesses to find solutions to their problems, and spending a lot of his time on the phone.

A programmer who used to answer to a project leader who answered directly to Alan Ashton and who felt he could go to Alan at any time, now works for a lead programmer, who works for a director, who works for a vice president, who works for a senior vice president, who works for Alan. He is taught to take his problems to his direct supervisor and not to go outside proper lines of authority or communication.

I am afraid that some of the changes are the result of throwing the bathwater out with the baby. After saying good-bye to me, there were a few people who didn't want to leave a single trace of me behind. Some of the changes seemed to be made only because someone wanted to do something differently from the way we did it when I was there. Most of the changes, however, are genuine attempts to put the customer first and do a good job for the new shareholders who enter the picture with the Initial Public Offering.

I had hoped that the public company version of WordPerfect Corporation would have been nearly identical to the private one. I hoped we could avoid going through an entire corporate makeover to satisfy the analysts and investment bankers. I was idealistic enough to think if we had to go with a lower stock price because of our strange way of doing things, that a few dollars here or there wouldn't matter. Since the original plan was to sell only 15 percent of the company, I couldn't see that it mattered much if the price was $15 a share instead of $20. What difference could $75 million make one way or the other when Bruce and Alan were still going to own stock worth well over $1 billion? I felt we could make the money back many times over if we could keep doing business the way we had in the past.

While I would like to think that my version of the company would do better than theirs, what matters most to the future of WordPerfect Corporation are its products. If WordPerfect for Windows 6.0 is a wonderful product, then the company will do very well for at least a few more years. Microsoft will no doubt outspend and outpromise WPCorp, but they cannot stop customers from desiring the best product. Even if Microsoft quotes lower prices, offers a more complete suite of products, promises more on-site attention, and avoids any FTC or Department of Justice action, WordPerfect Corporation can still win if they offer great products.

I hope WordPerfect Corporation also chooses to offer great service. One of the problems they face is their high head count. Their sales-per-employee ratio is not very good compared to those of their competition, so they are no doubt looking for ways to improve it. The new layers of management and the new employees working on new products are probably the biggest contributors to the low ratio, but these are not areas likely to be cut back. There are rumors that some customer support calls are going to be shifted to another company and that new limitations will be placed on the 800 number service in order to keep the customer support department from getting any bigger. There are also rumors that some permanent employees will be converted to temporary status, which will improve the head-count number, but won't make any real cuts. I hope they can sell enough product to justify their employee count, so they can avoid cutting back their services or hurting some of their employees.

My biggest regret in all my years at WordPerfect Corporation is that I didn't do a thorough enough job of teaching and explaining how I thought the company should be run. I was too involved in the day-to-day activities of the company to take the time to make sure our principles were defined and taught, or to explain the reasons behind all of the decisions I made. I thought good results would be enough to convince others that I knew what I was doing, but the good results only kept those who disagreed with me at bay. When sales went down, so did I. My fate was no different from that of anyone else who has had poor results when running a company owned by others.

If I had to do it all over again, I would have tried to find a way to either run the company officially, with the full support of Alan and Bruce, or shift some of my responsibilities to others. I took myself and my job too seriously. I held on to my opinions so strongly that I always put myself in a position where I had to shoulder too much of the blame. Someone had to say no, but it should have been someone else some of the time.

I admit I was a difficult person at times, but I could never find a way to run the business efficiently without disappointing a few people. If those who advise others have to work with a few more people than they can easily handle, and if everyone else has well-defined, important, and meaningful responsibilities, then everyone in the company has to work. Anyone who wants to take it easy and avoid their duties is bound to be unhappy. Anyone who wants to define their own principles and follow their own agenda is bound to get in trouble. There is simply no place to hide in a flat, well-run organization, when those who run the company are so close to those who do the work. There is also too much competition for a tall, poorly run organization to offer a permanent refuge for anyone, because that type of company will go out of business very quickly.

Although I have been critical of some of their decisions, I believe very strongly that Bruce and Alan have always tried and continue to do the best they can for their products, their customers, and their employees. I admire them for the great company they have built and for all the good they have done over the years. I hope that they and their employees will find a way to stay a few steps ahead of the fox. I cannot thank Bruce and Alan enough for giving me the chance to learn so much and have so much fun, and then for giving me my life back when it wasn't much fun any more.

# AFTERWORD

I have to admit that I wrote this book without a particular audience in mind, in much the same way we wrote some of our software at WordPerfect Corporation. Originally, I intended the audience to be WPCorp employees, to whom I would explain how I thought the company should work, but I didn't get very many pages written before I lost access to my readers. I continued to write anyway, driven by the project, unwilling to face the fact that few at WPCorp were still interested in my ideas. If nothing else, the project gave me an answer when my wife asked what I would do with the rest of my life. In the back of my mind, I thought writing this book would be worth the effort, if only to give my children and future grandchildren a chance to hear my version of the Word-Perfect story.

For those of you who read the book to figure out if WordPerfect stock is a good investment, I know I haven't given you a good answer. I frankly don't know. The software business is highly speculative and WordPerfect's primary competitor is very strong, but WPCorp has good employees and good products. If WPwin 6.0 is well received, the company has a good chance of maintaining sustainable growth. While I expect 6.0 will be a great product, I haven't seen it since I left the company, so I don't know for sure.

If you bought this book hoping to learn more about running a business, then I hope you remember the parts about teaching correct principles and allowing employees to govern themselves. In spite of the problems I had understanding and implementing this philosophy, I am convinced that it is the best way to run a business. In today's competitive environment, businesses can no longer afford the overhead of one supervisor for every five or six employees. As organizations flatten and supervision decreases, employees will have to make more decisions on their own and govern themselves much more than they have in the past. If a company is to function effectively, its employees must have a good understanding of what is expected of them. Very small organizations may be able to find success without defining and teaching correct principles, but any business with more than twenty-five or thirty people must get organized.

If the owners of a company were to pay me a large consulting fee to visit and analyze their organization, I would ask a few questions and offer some advice. To help summarize the ideas I have scattered throughout the book, I have used these last few pages to write down some questions and answers for a hypothetical company. This will not be a complete course in how to run a business, but it will cover the areas that I care about most and find most interesting.

**Question 1: Do all employees know who is running the company?** I don't think it matters much if you have one person or a small committee functioning as your chief executive officer, as long as everyone in the company knows and understands who is in charge. Your CEO should possess the following qualities: a vision of where the company is headed; the ability to communicate this vision effectively to those inside and outside the company; the temperament and patience to settle disagreements without creating dissension; a knowledge of finance that is sufficient to understand clearly how well or how poorly the company is doing; the ability to make good decisions within a reasonable amount of time; and a basic understanding of development, marketing, manufacturing, and the legal aspects of running the business. If the CEO is lacking in any of these areas—which is bound to be the case—then this person or committee needs to understand its deficiencies and know where to turn for help. If a small committee is used to govern a company, then its members should make their decisions unanimously rather than by a majority vote. It seems to me that the CEO should be of one mind, whether it be one person or a few persons acting as one.

**Question 2: Do all employees know why the company is in business and what it hopes to accomplish?** If they do not, then the person or persons running the business must define the purpose and objectives or goals, and communicate them to everyone in the company. Ideally, this information—along with the policies and procedures the company uses to conduct its business—should be written down, published, and distributed to all employees. Generally, a mission statement will accomplish much of this task, unless it is written to impress customers rather than help employees understand their jobs.

**Question 3: Is the organization structured efficiently?** To be certain a company is well structured, you should draw an organizational chart. This was something I resisted at WPCorp, because so many people got discouraged when they didn't see themselves at the top, and some people liked to think they worked for someone other than the person to whom they were supposed to report. I also didn't want to pay for a full-time employee to keep the chart up-to-date. If I were still there, however, I would complete at least one organizational chart. I would want to uncover areas of excessive hierarchy and areas with no hierarchy at all. I would start at the top and work my way down, asking people in the organization who worked for them. I would then reverse the process, working from the bottom up, asking people whom they worked for. I would check the personnel files to make sure no one was missing. It would be very enlightening to see if people's perceptions matched the supposed reality.

In practically every company I have visited, there is more hierarchy than those running it would like to admit. A department of a dozen people, which could get by with two layers—one for the supervisor and the other for the remaining eleven employees—can easily end up with four, if there is an assistant supervisor and a sub-level for assistants. Getting flat and staying that way requires constant vigilance.

**Question 4: Do all employees know and understand their duties?** The best way to ensure this is to give all employees, including the board members and the CEO, a written job description. In my ideal company, each job description would contain the purpose and objectives of the position, and the sum of all the individual job descriptions would equal the company's purpose and objectives.

Every job in the company should be defined in the broadest possible terms, so that all employees could make a significant contribution to the enterprise. For example, a receptionist's job might be narrowly defined, with a purpose of greeting visitors and answering the phone, and objectives of preventing unwanted visitors, answering every phone call quickly, and keeping track of the comings and goings of everyone in the company.

The job could, however, become much more meaningful if the purpose was to protect the security of the company while making sure all visitors and callers felt welcome. The objectives could be to give all visitors proper attention and help, to make sure all callers receive prompt and courteous attention, and to know where employees are so visitors and callers won't be kept waiting.

**Question 5: Do all your employees receive proper training?** In many companies, employees are thrown into jobs untrained, having only one chance to sink or swim. This is an awful waste of resources. All employees deserve good initial and ongoing training. At a minimum, they deserve to meet with their advisors twice a year (I would try for four times) to review their job descriptions and learn what they are doing well and what they are doing poorly. The company owes them sufficient training and support to ensure they have a reasonable chance to do a good job.

Advisors need training as well. They should be taught to be kind, courteous, and respectful when working with the people they advise. They need to be taught not to intimidate their workers when they feel threatened or insecure. They must learn not only to praise their people, but also to reprove them with clarity when they do something wrong.

**Question 6: Are all employees accountable to their job descriptions and to the purpose, objectives, policies, and procedures of the company?** In my experience, it has been much easier to turn people loose than it has been to turn them loose and hold them accountable. Accountability is essential, since correct principles and the best training are of no value if employees don't follow what they are taught. While most advisors do fairly well at patting people on the back when they do something right, few are good at communicating clearly when someone does something wrong. An advisor who can reprove without

upsetting an employee more than is necessary is someone you want to keep in your organization.

**Question 7: Do employees work together?** Employees
should be on the same page of the same script, all working to do their best. They should know their parts and
should perform them at the right time. For a company
to be as effective as possible, people have to work together as a team rather than as individuals. If employees
go off in their own directions, with their own agendas,
working only for their own gratification, the company
will go nowhere.

**Question 8: Are all employees allowed to communicate
their problems and questions with anyone in the company?** I don't like to see mistakes repeated that result
from poor communication within a company. I strongly
dislike the practice of prohibiting employees who occupy the lowest positions in an organization from speak-
ing to those who occupy the highest. I believe very
strongly that anyone in a company should be allowed to
communicate with anyone else, even if that lets a custo-
dian communicate directly with the CEO. This does not
mean that employees should be given an hour-long appointment with the president any time they wish, but
they should be allowed to send e-mail messages or notes
to the president when no one else will listen to them.
The light needs to shine everywhere in a company, and
advisors should not be allowed to use their employees'
loyalty or strictly enforced lines of communication to
protect their domain from scrutiny or accountability.

**Question 9: Is the company living within the limits of
its cash flow?** Too many companies postpone the day
when they will show a reasonable profit. Some charge too
little for their products and services; others overspend.
While excuses like "We have to spend more now because
our window of opportunity is about to close," or "We
have to charge less to keep up with our competition," may

seem reasonable, I do not think they are. If your company has no cash flow, then you need to get one before you burn through too much investor money. If you have a cash flow, then you need to show a profit. If you can't find a way to show a profit, then you need to cut your losses and close down your business.

**Question 10: Do you try whenever possible to choose the simple rather than the complex solution?** Business is a fairly simple activity. You identify a need, figure out how to fill it, manufacture your solution, and find the best way to sell your product at a profit. You then support your customers with reliable service consistent with the price you charge, make sure you collect your money, and pay your taxes on time. After that, you listen to your customers, and based on what they tell you and whatever else you figure out, you improve your product as fast as you can to stay ahead of your competition. All the other things, like strategic alliances, weird pricing and promotional schemes, and trying to create needs when they do not exist, introduce complexities that never help in the long run. I never found an occasion when the complex solution was better than the simple one.

A company that can answer yes to these ten questions can accomplish incredible feats. If everyone is focused on the same objectives, all possessing proper training, trust, and accountability, and if the company can live within its means and keep things simple, I believe it can do anything it wants to do.

# INDEX